The Unique and Universal Christ

The Unique and Universal Christ

Jesus in a Plural World

Michael Nazir-Ali

Paternoster:
thinking faith

MILTON KEYNES ● COLORADO SPRINGS ● HYDERABAD

14 13 12 11 10 09 08   7 6 5 4 3 2 1

First published 2008 by Paternoster
Paternoster is an imprint of Authentic Media
9 Holdom Avenue, Bletchley, Milton Keynes, Bucks, MK1 1QR, UK
1820 Jet Stream Drive, Colorado Springs, CO 80921, USA
OM Authentic Media, Medchal Road, Jeedimetla Village,
Secunderabad 500 055, A.P., India
www.authenticmedia.co.uk

Authentic Media is a division of IBS-STL U.K., limited by guarantee, with its
Registered Office at Kingstown Broadway, Carlisle, Cumbria CA3 0HA.
Registered in England & Wales No. 1216232. Registered charity 270162

British Library Cataloguing in Publication Data

A catalogue record for this book is available from the British Library

ISBN-13: 978-1-84227-551-1

Design by James Kessel for Scratch the Sky Ltd (www.scratchthesky.com)
Print Management by Adare
Printed and bound in Great Britain by J.H. Haynes & Co., Sparkford

Contents

Foreword

Thirty years ago I was on a train returning from London to Southgate when I got into a deep conversation with a stranger. Perhaps it was my clerical collar that originated it. From the weather we moved to politics, then on to values and then, finally, to religion. He said how much he respected the teaching of Jesus and what a great man he was. I then remarked that the greatness of Jesus lay not in his humanity but in what followers of Jesus Christ call his relationship with God and in his resurrection. The atmosphere between us suddenly changed. He seemed to recoil and he said curtly: 'On that matter, we must part company', and he left the train.

If anything, thirty years on, the situation is more demanding, and the pressure on Christian people to conform to opinions formed by secular culture more insidious. The 'liberal Jesus' is already a recognizable type formed by cultures that reject ideas of miracles, answered prayer and a personal God. Long ago Richard Niebuhr attacked liberal Protestantism for teaching that 'a God without wrath brought men without sin into a kingdom without judgement through the ministrations of a Christ without a cross'. Sadly, Niebuhr's indictment is more applicable now than it has ever been. Sermons are frequently preached where Jesus is portrayed as little more than a superior kind of being, closer, perhaps, to a successful social worker than to the Son of God. Such representations sit uncomfortably with the received teaching of a Saviour whose work on the cross redeems human-kind and establishes a new relationship with God. Proponents of the liberal Jesus are in such thrall to modernity that they do not perceive how much they are shackled by their culture.

A newer form of the problem is one created by the inter-religious age that is part of western culture. Our anxiety to accept other faiths as co-equal with our own has led to the downgrading of Christology. The 'Jewish Jesus' and the 'Muslim Christ' have many insights to share with us, but the desire of some Christians not to hurt or shock people of other faiths, or their wish not to seem intolerant, has led to a Christological reductionism that falls far short of traditional teaching. We therefore are no longer shocked to see Eucharistic liturgies where Mohammed or Moses appears alongside Christ as co-redeemer of humankind.

It is to this bewildering market place of competing faiths, clashing cultures and alternative religions that Bishop Michael Nazir-Ali's distillation of his 2007 Chavasse Lectures comes as a welcome contribution that is both brilliant and healing. After a careful and detailed examination of the current situation and the conforming pressure of culture, he shows that the Church's traditional teaching has enormous power to heal the brokenness of humanity, and to be a bridge between different cultures. With respect and sensitivity Dr Nazir-Ali probes concepts of Jesus in Judaism, Hinduism and Islam, and shows that failure to present the fullness of teaching about Jesus Christ does not contribute towards genuine dialogue but rather denies it.

It is my expectation that Dr Nazir-Ali's exploration of the uniqueness of Jesus Christ within modern culture will encourage debate and further study not only in Christian congregations but between faiths. Most readers of this book will have little difficulty in echoing Pope Benedict's words expressed in his *Jesus of Nazareth* that 'the Christological dimension – in other words, the mystery of the Son as revealer of the Father – is present in everything Jesus says and does'. Discovery of this truth, so powerfully presented in Michael Nazir-Ali's book, has the potential to reactivate Christian mission as well as confident dialogue with those who disagree.

Lord Carey of Clifton
Archbishop of Canterbury 1991–2002

By Way of an Introduction

In every age, and in many cultures, people have asked what Jesus of Nazareth has to do with the opportunities, problems and questions with which they are faced. Such issues have been of an 'ultimate' kind about the significance of the person or the destiny of the universe but, equally, they have also been about the changes, chances and choices of everyday living. How should different groups of people be treated in society? What respect is due to the person and what is the balance between individual freedoms and social obligations? Should the State be informed by a particular set of moral and spiritual principles or should it have a minimal role in ordering relationships between competing interests? What is the relationship between divine revelation and human experience and how does it work out in the contribution that the followers of Jesus seek to make in the public sphere?

Our age is no different except, perhaps, in the rapid rate of change with which we have to deal, whether in the realm of technological development or in what is socially acceptable – which alters almost from day to day under pressure of alleged 'new' knowledge, the seduction of life-changing 'therapies' or the lifestyles to which we have become accustomed. The Christian tradition can, of course, relate positively to some of these changes. If we hold to a strong doctrine of creation, we will not be surprised by the ways in which the world is capable of being understood by the human mind nor, indeed, will the technological use of such knowledge be unexpected. Other changes, however, will cause concern and may even have to be opposed in the name of Jesus. Increasingly characteristic of our society is a self-regard that goes beyond the legitimate respect we ought to have for ourselves as beings made in God's image. Such selfishness is sometimes dressed up as self-fulfilment, whether in the pampering of the body, in a disregard for commitment in relationships or in the patching together of a pick 'n' mix spirituality whereby individuals satisfy their own needs without much thought for neighbour or wider society.[1]

The tendency towards a pick 'n' mix spirituality arises out of a sense that all faiths are, at bottom, the same and that it is, therefore, legitimate to pick out bits and pieces from all of them for the construction of a personal spirituality. Such attitudes also have repercussions in wider society where 'faith' is often thought of as an undifferentiated 'something or other', which all people in the faith communities have and which can be catered for regardless of distinctions between one faith and another. 'Sacred space', for example, can be shared without scruple, even if its initial dedication had been Christian; chaplains must facilitate worship for those of other faiths, even when this is against their conscience; and community facilities can only be made available for 'multi-faith' use.

In addition to selfishness, syncretism, or the desire to unite all religious traditions, whether for the sake of a personalized spirituality or for social reasons, has to be confronted and rejected in the name of God's unique self-disclosure in Jesus Christ.

Each culture, and the different ages, are characterized by specific wrongs, sins or shortcomings, whatever you want to call them. In some, it is an inordinate love of money and wealth generally, which leads to rampant corruption. In others, it is the chauvinistic glorifying of a tribe, an ethnic group or a national identify in such a way that it brings about discrimination and conflict. In the contemporary west, however, the besetting sin or the pervasive disorder has to do with sexual permissiveness or licence. No relationship is sacrosanct and Aphrodite is the reigning goddess. The stability and flourishing of the family, the proper maturing of the young, which comes from relating to each parent in a particular way, the management of sexually-transmitted diseases and even matters of public order are all related in one way or another to the changing sexual mores of a society. Once again, we have to ask what the relevance of Jesus is to such a situation and, more generally, to the 'fallen' aspects of any and every culture.

Like many others, I have long pondered over these matters and have come to the conclusion that a proper view of the uniqueness of God's revelation in Christ and its universal significance must be at the start, and at the heart, of Christian responses to this complex and ever-changing world that we inhabit.

An opportunity to address these matters in a reasonably systematic way came when I was invited to deliver the 2007 Chavasse Lectures at Wycliffe Hall, Oxford. I feel immensely privileged to have been asked to do these lectures. First of all, because they are in honour of Bishop Christopher Chavasse, a distinguished mission-minded Bishop of Rochester, and his father, Bishop Francis Chavasse, an equally distinguished Bishop of Liverpool and, at one time, Principal of Wycliffe Hall. The Chavasse family is greatly admired in the Church and beyond for their courage, creativity and, above all, fidelity to the gospel. Having lived for so long in Bishop Christopher's shadow, I offer these lectures in gratitude for all his sowing of the Word from which I, and so many others, have benefited.

Another reason for feeling privileged is that so many of my great predecessors at the Church Mission Society have also been Chavasse lecturers. I need mention only John V. Taylor, Simon Barrington-Ward and Douglas Webster. Others have been mentors and teachers and yet others friends, of whose friendship I am hardly worthy. I thank God for them all.

In these lectures I have tried to show how the fundamental values and virtues that are needed today for human flourishing arise from a Christian vision that has to do with the person and work of Jesus Christ. I have, naturally, given some attention to what an adequate doctrine of Christ's person might be in the light of the present-day challenges faced by Christians and the Church. I have also considered how the work of Christ enables that new start with God and with ourselves that we must make if there is to be any personal and social transformation. I have then gone on to consider the different views that have been held on the ways in which Christ relates to culture, and have suggested that the gospel both affirms God-given aspects of every culture and also says a clear 'no' to those that have to do with our fallenness. I have looked at the particular case of the gospel's relationship to people of different faiths and, to some extent, the faiths themselves. Once again, I have tried to set out the positive relationships that there can be but from a position of holding on to the distinctiveness of the Christian faith. Finally, I have made an attempt to draw out the implications for mission if we set Jesus Christ at the centre of our engagement with the world around us and consider the Church's calling from such a perspective.

Because each chapter, more or less, has been a lecture, I have been limited in the material I have been able to use and the subjects I have been able to address. I have, however, at least some of the time, indicated where additional information is available.

I am very grateful to Dawn Saxton, my former secretary, and to Karina Shuter for typing the manuscript and, as always, to my family for tolerating yet another intrusion into family time and even family holidays.

May Jesus Christ be praised and this sinner forgiven!

+Michael Nazir-Ali
Pentecost, 2008

1

Fundamental Values and Jesus of Nazareth

Everybody wants values: education authorities state that children should be secure in their values, commercial organizations wish to be known for their right values and universities flaunt the values they have for teaching and learning. Such concern for values is a good sign. It shows that the culture and its governing structures want more than a brute market for the exchange of goods and services, more than just coercive arrangements for maintaining law and order, more even than what is offered by the tyranny of an elective dictatorship, which democracy can so easily become.

What are these values that everyone wishes to have? They can be expressed in a number of ways and will, of course, be different for different institutions and people. There are, however, some core values that become immediately apparent as we consider our life together. There is, first of all, a desire to affirm human *dignity* and a sense that once it is recognized in an individual or a group, it cannot be taken away. Then there is the notion of *liberty*, the belief that all human beings have been created free and, as the American Declaration of Independence puts it, that it is the duty of governments to protect and uphold such freedom. Not only are people free, but they are also equal before the law. The notion of *equality* is one of the principal values underlying legislation today. Finally, there is the requirement of *safety*: people need to be protected from harm, whether it be inflicted by crime, professional neglect or the failure of local, regional or national government. In contemporary western societies, this protection from harm is often interpreted individualistically but it is very far from certain that its scope is not much wider and includes harm to vital social institutions such as marriage, family or even the Church.[1]

In this connection, it is interesting to note what the various declarations say about these core values. The Declaration of Independence speaks of the inalienable right to life, liberty and the pursuit of happiness, while the UN Declaration of Human Rights recognizes that the inherent dignity and the equal and inalienable rights of all members of the human family are the foundation of freedom, justice and peace in the world. The abortive Constitution for Europe also speaks of inviolable and inalienable rights and in doing this it is simply echoing the European Convention on Human Rights. Colin Chapman has, by the way, pointed out the significant differences that are to be found between such internationally-recognized declarations and the declarations that have been made from time to time by bodies such as the Islamic Council of Europe and the Organization of the Islamic Conference. He writes that there are fundamental tensions on matters of equality, freedom and dignity. In Muslim society, non-Muslims and women are manifestly *not* equal in the sense set out in the UN Declaration. Freedom of expression, of belief and freedom to change one's belief are not fully recognized and, in the area of penal law, certain Islamic punishments cannot be seen to respect human dignity.[2]

The question that faces us is whether the values that are cherished by an emerging global civilization are free-standing. Did they suddenly arise from the Enlightenment in eighteenth-century Europe or have they roots that are deeper than that? Why should these values, as the American Declaration of Independence claims, be 'self-evident'? If they are not to be simply imposed on an unwilling world by an 'enlightened elite', they must be shown to cohere with, and even arise out of, what people believe about themselves and the world in which they live.

Nor are these values simply a matter of personal morality and conduct. They have profoundly to do with policy-making, legislation and government. They are not even just about how individuals behave socially. They have necessarily to be also about social, economic and political institutions. A famous politician once said to me, 'Morality we leave to the bishops!' As a bishop, I had to say, 'No, thank you.' Morality is too important to be left to bishops and other clergy. Properly understood, it is too important to be left to the individual and it certainly should not be left simply to the politicians. The values we have been discussing have to be understood and held by all. We should all know from where they have arisen and why we hold them.

In the last few years in Parliament those proposing and opposing new legislation on a number of important issues have had to face demands to justify the values they have invoked. For instance, any move to legalize euthanasia or assisted suicide immediately raises issues about the inherent dignity or value of human beings. Can we ever say that disease has reached a point where life no longer has value and can be brought to an end either by the patient or by a medical practitioner? Similar questions are raised about mental impairment. Is it ever possible to say that a lack of mental capacity renders a person without inherent dignity?[3] In any case, on what basis do we speak at all of human dignity?

When such matters are raised, legislators and moral philosophers often invoke a transcendent principle. Thus, even agnostic philosophers have said that, in the end, notions of inherent human dignity depend on the Judaeo-Christian view that men and women have been created in God's image and that this can never be taken away from them. This means that except in self-defence, or to protect society as a whole, human life must not be taken, though, of course, people should be and are enabled to die in dignity and with as little pain as possible.

What is significant for end-of-life issues is also important when thinking about the beginning of life. At this stage, the most important question is: When is there a human person? Is it at the time of conception, when all the genetic material required is in place, or should there be a developmental notion of person-hood, which takes into account not only genetics, but also the relational, the sentient and the neurological aspects of a foetus' development? Naturally, the relationship with the mother is of crucial importance and thus the implantation of the embryo in the womb is a landmark event. Pictures on television have shown us how the foetus can indicate sentience at an early stage and this, together with the establishing of the 'nerve-net' and the beginning of brain activity, have for long been criteria for thinking about personhood in relation to the foetus.[4] When I served as chair of the Ethics and Law Committee of the Human Fertilisation and Embryology Authority, I began to see, however, that the question of personhood could never be settled simply on biological grounds. As Robert Song points out, this is a moral issue although, of course, scientific data must be taken into account. I was driven more and more to the conclusion that while personhood *is* a developmental matter, we cannot know for certain when the definitive beginnings are and different people will continue to see them at different stages of foetal development. The prudential course, therefore, is to regard the embryo/foetus as if it were a person from the earliest stages. My other response was more and more to follow a path that would cause the least evil, for example, by minimizing wastage or destruction of embryos in particular procedures or by requiring that embryos should not be created solely for research. As can be imagined, neither of these stances was universally popular in that context!

The question about the beginning of personhood is important, of course, because 'inalienable dignity' is ascribed to the embryo or foetus from whatever stage it is recognized as having personhood. The earlier this is seen as happening, or even being possible, the more restricted the scope for experimentation, manipulation and termination. If we feel we must regard the embryo or foetus as personal from its earliest stages, then we invest it from the beginning with human dignity – and for those who derive their values from the Bible, this is about people being in the image of God.

In the debates on equality legislation, questions have sometimes been raised about our basis for thinking that human beings of different races, genders, ages and social status should be equal before the law. Once again, the answer that lawyers, not known for their practice of the Christian faith, have given is that such notions of fundamental equality go back to Christian origins. Values such as dignity and equality are not free-standing. We cannot just pluck them from the air and make a list of them to assist us in forming the young or in promoting legislation. Such an eclectic approach would be dangerous because if they are regarded discretely in this way, they may just wither. We would then be left only with a crude form of utilitarianism (does this work for the majority?) or with public opinion (with its ever-changing and media-manipulated 'yuk' factor). There are disturbing signs that this is happening already.

An eclectic and vestigial view of values would also lack integrity. It would be saying, in effect, that we want to hold on to some of these values but we do not want the system or the world view from which they have emerged because it is inconvenient and/or outdated. This is sometimes the view taken of the relationship of Christianity to leading values in our culture today.[5] We are beginning to appreciate, however, that basic values are deeply embedded in a moral and spiritual *vision*. This means that the Christian understanding and the values we believe to be important derive their strength and, indeed, their meaning from the vision that gave rise to them and they cannot flourish without it.

For Christians, then, human dignity is not just vestigially connected to some vague teaching about being made in God's image. It receives its vigour from all that God has disclosed of his purposes for us in the resurrection of Jesus Christ from the dead. It is this event that both affirms and vindicates the whole of creation, but especially the creation of humanity in God's image. It looks forward to the *telos*, or end, for which we have been created, and manifests what that is to be. The resurrection is about the redemption of the universe as a whole but also about the saving and the destiny of humanity (Rom. 8:18–25). This aspect of the Christian vision not only provides teleological meaning for individual women and men, and for humanity in general, but also gives us the means of valuing the whole of creation, which is being transformed by the will of the Creator.[6] We must, of course, give close attention to science and the ways in which it helps us to wonder at and about the universe but science cannot and should not remove from the horizon questions about personal and universal meaning.

Similarly, equality is rooted in the vision that sees human difference not so much destroyed as transcended in Christ. When Galatians 3:28 tells us that there is 'neither Jew nor Greek, slave nor free, male nor female' in Christ, it does not mean there is no difference but that differences do not matter as far as belonging to this new reality is concerned. Elsewhere, St Paul is quite prepared to see the special vocation of the Jewish people and how this relates to the Church's universal mission (Rom. 9 –11). Christian belief in the fundamental equality of men and women does not exempt us from acknowledging both sameness and difference; the common mission given to humanity in Genesis 1:26–28 is to be fulfilled in different ways, but fulfilled together. There is both mutuality and order in the blessed Trinity and this is reflected in creation and in human society. This means that ontological equality and diversity of vocation and mission can be held together. Equality does not mean uniformity, nor does unity.

We have recently been celebrating the bicentenary of the abolition of the slave trade. Those evangelical and other Christians who campaigned against this evil based their campaign precisely on the gospel value of equality but they also knew the difference in power relations between slave and free, between the powerful and the powerless. They wanted the slaves to be free so that they could be authentically what God wanted them to be and that was certainly not exactly like the slavers who had taken them captive![7]

In the Christian vision, then, both dignity and equality are taken to a new level: innate human dignity is not only recognized, but is also restored in the resurrection and exalted in the ascension. The practical results of these events have to do with persons being conscious anew of their place in God's purposes and of their ultimate destiny. It is not an accident that the receiving of the gospel by groups of oppressed and marginalized people has given them not only the dignity of which they had been deprived, but also a sense of destiny, of being able to make a difference to the course of history.[8] Equality, similarly, has to do with finding an identity in the new thing that God is doing in Christ – breaking down barriers, enmities and difference so that a new kind of humanity might emerge from the old.

Such an identity is both affirming and transforming. Instead of seeing themselves as 'nobodies', the poor now know they are 'somebody' in God's eyes. This leads to radical change in their ways of living, their attitudes to education and work, the amount of time given to the family and the status of women in society.[9]

What can we say about liberty? True Christian freedom is, of course, about finding ourselves, at the deepest level, to be in accord with the divine moral law. This is a gift from God that rights our wrong and sets us on a new path of worship and obedience – 'whose service is perfect freedom', the Book of Common Prayer calls it, meaning by 'service', as does the Bible, both worship and obedience.

Obedience to God can, however, lead to disobedience to other authorities if God's rights are being usurped. It is for this reason that the apostles refused to obey the religious authorities of their day, declaring, 'We must obey God rather than men!' (Acts 5:29). For the same reason, the early Christians refused to sacrifice to the emperors when they claimed to be *'dominus et deus'*.[10] This led to several periods of systematic persecution and martyrdom. Ironically, at about the time of their emancipation in the Roman Empire, Christians were subjected to a violent persecution under the Persian emperor Shapur II, for very similar reasons.[11] In the course of history such acts of radical obedience (or disobedience, depending on our point of view) have, in fact, led to greater political and religious freedom. Such, for example, is the history of Puritan settlements in North America. Fleeing persecution from the established Church, the Pilgrim Fathers and others found more freedom in the land of their adoption.[12] Gradually, of course, more from expediency than principle, toleration spread even in Europe. Given the firmness of conviction it was, in some cases, the only way to maintain national unity.

In this connection, it is interesting that in an address to the American people given at the beginning of his presidency, President Khatami of Iran highlights the connection between the religious beliefs of the Puritans and their love of freedom. According to him, the Puritans desired a system that related their worship of God to human dignity and freedom. Under the

Puritan system, liberty found in religion a cradle for its growth and religion found protection of liberty as its divine calling. The United States, he goes on to say, has departed from such a spiritual and moral vision and therein lies the source of its own malaise as well as its baleful influence in international affairs. In this address, the former President shows a remarkable grasp of American history. Americans might well say to him, 'Physician, heal thyself!' and it is certainly true that he failed to deliver on his reforming manifesto, but nevertheless, the link he makes between the radical religion of the Puritans and the value of liberty is difficult to deny.[13] At the heart of the Puritan understanding of liberty was a central Reformation insight that all Christians could and should read the Bible for themselves so that they could order their personal and social lives by its teaching. Christian notions of personal responsibility and of accountability before God have certainly played their part in the emergence of ideas of personal freedom.

Until the Second Vatican Council, the Roman Catholic Church had little teaching on religious freedom, especially for those who were thought to be in grave error (error has no rights). This Council, however, in its Declaration on Religious Liberty, *Dignitatis Humanae*, taught that in order to seek the truth and to adhere to it, human beings needed to be free, both within themselves and from external constraint. Only in this way could their adherence to the truth be in accord with their own natures. Such freedom had to do, therefore, with human nature itself and it must not be taken away, save only for the sake of public order.[14]

'If the Son sets you free, you will be free indeed' (John 8:36). The freedom that Jesus brings is not a release from our obligations nor is it permission to do whatever we please. It has to do, rather, with receiving strength to adhere to the moral law. Such adherence will never be perfect by any means and the struggle between flesh and spirit continues throughout the Christian life (Rom. 7:13–25) but gradually, and astonishingly, in Christ we become the righteousness of God (2 Cor. 5:21). This Christian insight was put in secular form by Immanuel Kant when he taught that authentic freedom is about keeping the moral law. In fact, humanity's obligation to keep the moral law requires freedom. Whatever may have been Kant's motivation and whatever his desire to escape from authority, his formulation owes everything to Christian understandings of freedom, law and duty – except, of course, Christian reliance on grace in keeping the moral law.[15] Such a view of freedom safeguards us from purely rights-based approaches that emphasize individual liberty over other considerations. The discussion of rights can be based on important Christian truths, such as the *imago dei* and its renewal, or God's covenantal relationship with humanity, but it also has to be firmly placed, as Joan O'Donovan has argued, in the context of a just ordering of human community with the mutual obligations inherent in such an understanding. This issue must not merely be viewed in a voluntarist, individualist and subjectivist way.[16]

In some kitchens the other day I saw a sign that said, 'Health and Safety Rule OK'. Considerations of health and safety are becoming more and more prominent in every aspect of our lives – commercial, domestic and leisure. Very often, it has to be said, the motivation is not so much concern for our safety as the desire of our employers or those who supply us with goods and services to be protected from possible legal action. Once again, the biblical view is much wider, being based on the notion of *shalom*, which means not only safety, but also completeness, soundness and welfare. It includes physical safety but is also concerned with mental and spiritual well-being. It is about the individual but in the context of the welfare of the whole community. It is the basis for thinking holistically about ourselves and the world in which we live. In the New Testament, similarly, *sozein* can mean preservation or deliverance from danger, disease or death but its dominant meaning rapidly becomes that of spiritual salvation and has to do more and more with eternal destiny. It should be noted that salvation in the Bible is about freedom from internal or external limitation and can have both individual and communal reference. The latter is important for our day: as we have seen, so much talk about safety from harm is based on saving individuals from the harm that others may cause them, whether these are persons or organizations, but we should also be concerned about social harm to those institutions without which society cannot flourish.

Just as values are integrally related to vision, so are the virtues that make up our characters. Character is about the kind of people we are and it determines how we behave in public and in private. A virtuous character will act consistently in the public and private spheres. There can be differences of approach but no dichotomy between the two. How we behave in private will have implications for our public role and its responsibilities, and vice versa.

Some virtues, such as wisdom, courage, generosity and justice, have been widely recognized since ancient times as being about the proper development of the human person. A mature person who did not manifest them sufficiently would be regarded as lacking in some important attributes. In addition to these, Christianity has brought the distinctive theological virtues of faith, hope and love. These are bestowed on us by God and are particularly inculcated within the fellowship of God's people, the Church. It has to be said, however, that even the 'natural' virtues will be seen and received by Christians in distinctive ways: the fear of God will be seen as the true foundation of wisdom; courage will be understood in terms of Jesus' acceptance of the cross and his call for us also to take up our crosses and to follow him; justice will be interpreted in terms of God's demand on us and not simply of what is currently fashionable in our society; generosity will spring from our own thankfulness for all that God has done for us.

Alasdair MacIntyre has drawn our attention to the importance of relating virtues to a moral and spiritual system. His thesis is that we live at a time when only discrete fragments of such a system survive and that even this may be giving way to an all-enveloping darkness. His recipe is to advocate the emergence of distinct and distinctive moral and spiritual communities where the vision, the virtues and the values can be nurtured. This is how the Benedictines and other religious communities contributed to the survival of civilization through the Dark Ages.[17] If what he is saying is correct, then churches, particularly in the west, need to move from patterns of 'working with the grain', of being part of the social furniture, to being radically alternative communities where the leading evangelical metaphor is not 'salt' but 'light'. Rather than being dispersed in society and working invisibly within the existing social order, Christians have to model communities of vision that create character and produce values in ways that have integrity and wholeness. Here there will be no free-standing values and no virtues that have been picked out simply to assist in programmes of self-fulfilment. There will, rather, be a controlling vision of what is good for us and for the world in which we live.

Personal and social life that springs from vision, in which certain virtues have been instilled and which holds to particular values, will be life that is *vectorial*, that is, it will be life with direction. At the time of the millennium, a leading Jewish rabbi pointed out the debt that the world owed the Jewish people for the modern conception of time. While many, if not all, ancient cultures continued to view time as cyclical, with a coming to be and a passing away that are endlessly repeated, the Bible portrays time as linear. It begins with God's eternal purposes as expressed in the creation of the universe and it is moving towards the great denouement, the fulfilment of God's will for the universe. Such a conception of time is vital to scientific theory, to our understanding of history and to the ordering of our personal and collective lives. Out of all proportion to their numbers, the Jews have made, and continue to make, an enormous spiritual, moral and intellectual contribution to human civilization. For all of this, we owe them a considerable debt of gratitude.[18]

But although the theological view of time, which is so characteristic of the Bible, was mediated by the Jews, it has been to a very large extent the Christian Church that has owned it, elaborated on it and spread it round the world as an aspect of its global mission.[19] The Church sees all sacred history leading to definition, fulfilment and completion in the person and work of Jesus Christ. The story of the Church itself is then understood as working towards the appearance (*parousia*) of the Lord, when he will 'recapitulate' in himself all things, whether in heaven or on earth (Eph. 1:10). In this he is revealed both as the source of all things and also their final destiny, as Alpha but also Omega (Col. 1:15–20).

It is this view of time that has made it possible for us to see the universe and, indeed, life itself in an evolutionary light. A view of time that is genuinely open or 'epigenetic' has made history both possible and interesting. It is important, however, not to forget that a properly biblical view of time is also teleological, that is to say, it has to do with purpose and direction, and not only of grand themes such as the destiny of the universe and the course of human history, but also of each one of us –we are a crucial and unique part of the story. But it is not just about us. We are part of a providential plan for the world. We are not, therefore, creatures who crave for meaning in a meaningless universe, we do not simply construct our own meaning in the wastes and voids of an indifferent and even hostile world, but the rest of the universe responds to our quest for knowledge, order and predictability. It is this that allows us to situate our own sense of meaning and direction within the wider picture. Even when there is disorder, catastrophe and cruelty, we know they are not part of God's ultimate purpose for his world. There is a tendency towards organization rather than disorganization, towards order rather than disorder, towards beauty and simplicity rather than wasteful tangledness and ugliness. It is entirely right, of course, for science to seek explanations for phenomena by investigating cause and effect. It is equally understandable for historians to consider events and consequences. Neither science nor history, however, should be seen as a way of evading questions about teleology – personal, social or even universal.

As Rick Warren has pointed out, we have been made for friendship with God, to worship and to serve him, to become more and more like Christ so that God's power can work in us and through us. Such a plan depends wholly on God's initiative and sustaining, of course, but it also has to do with our response, a response that is not made on our own but in the company of all of those who have responded to what God is doing for us in Christ and who seek to remain faithful and trusting in God's leading and guidance.[20]

As we have been saying, it is important not only for individuals or groups to have a vision that provides the driving force for their lives, but also for societies and nations. 'Where there is no vision, the people perish,' the Bible says (Prov. 29:18, AV) and it may be important to remember that the word here translated 'vision' also means 'revelation'. In other words, it is not just that we construct any vision for ourselves but that it has to come from all that God has shown us about himself and about our world. It is not, of course, that things are good or bad just because God has said so. It is, rather, that God's revealed truth casts a flood of light on who we are and how we are, on what the rest of creation is like and what makes for its and our well-being and wholeness.

For many centuries, the UK, like many other nations, sought to order its social, political and economic life by the Christian vision. For an observer, it is impossible to imagine how, without the benefit of Christianity, so many disparate people – Celts, Picts, Anglo-Saxons, Danes, etc. – who were often in conflict with one another, could have come together to form a single, great and united kingdom. Most of the great buildings, even 'secular' ones, the art and the music owe everything to Christian beliefs and values. It has often been pointed out that Tyndale's, and subsequent, translations of the Bible into English both triggered and underlie the development of the English language and the emergence of great prose and poetry. Shakespeare (or Milton or Herbert or Donne) is unimaginable without Tyndale.[21]

The essence of the British constitution remains 'the Queen in Parliament under God'. The emergence of parliamentary institutions, the development of law, and particularly the notion of civil liberties, the judicial system and other customs associated with government, all took place under Christian inspiration. But having said this, several points need to be noted immediately. First, the Christian vision informing personal or social values was sometimes distorted. It was made to serve a rigid class system, for example, or to justify imperial adventure. It was also used to create oppressive patterns of the family, far removed from Jesus' teaching on marriage as a creation ordinance. Such patterns were sometimes particularly difficult for women and children.

Secondly, we need to acknowledge that the Enlightenment appropriated and clarified many of the ideas inherent in

Christian tradition. The values of liberty, of duty as well as right, of justice and of equality were made central to Enlightenment humanism. The Enlightenment, however, also, and notoriously, relegated religion to the private sphere. It is claimed that this happened because religion had played a part in the endemic conflicts of Europe in the seventeenth and eighteenth centuries and the only way to obtain a lasting peace was, therefore, to banish religion from public discourse altogether. Apart from the fact that it is far from clear that religion was the only, or even the most important, cause of these wars, the results of this banishing have been most serious for many western societies. Some philosophers, for instance, Immanuel Kant, tried to secularize moral discourse, but even so, God had to be invoked as a regulative idea.[22] Others, as we have seen, wanted to hang on to Christian values without the faith that gave rise to them. The net result of all of these attempts at moral reconstruction has been to deprive the fundamental values of the Enlightenment of their spiritual, moral and rational basis. This is why moral philosophers, when they are not reflecting public opinion or commending utility, but are seeking to justify fundamental values such as dignity or equality, seem to invoke transcendental notions that appear from nowhere.

I have already referred to the pick 'n' mix mentality: people today are quite willing and able to construct their world view, ideas of personal destiny and spirituality from the array of options that are now available to them. Such options come from a bewildering variety of sources: religions of Indian origin, such as Hinduism or Buddhism, nature mysticism, pantheism or monism, mystical traditions within Judaism, Christianity or Islam and ideas that come from popular mythology. The overriding aim of such spiritualities is personal fulfilment and well-being.[23] Where social morality is concerned, however, there are two opposing tendencies to note. On the one hand, Christian ideas of monogamy, of family responsibility, of social responsibility for the poor, needy and the stranger, remain stubbornly entrenched. A schools marriage project, for instance, continues to discover nearly universal belief among school-children in the life-long nature of marriage. On the other hand, however, government policy is increasingly not to privilege Christianity in any way. This is done on two counts. There is the formal argument that to do so would be to run up against anti-discrimination legislation. The other is the plea that we are a multi-faith society and to acknowledge the special place of one faith would be to marginalize the others. It is maintained that all legislative, executive and judicial decisions must be made in the light of such considerations.

It has to be said at once that such claims are not often made by people (or even leaders) of the non-Christian faiths. They are, on the whole, glad if Christianity's role is acknowledged in the public sphere since this can mean that spiritual considerations have a place in policy-making, and this is good and desirable. What they would like Christians to do is to help provide a place for them so that they too can have their say.[24]

Who, then, is making these claims about multi-faith issues? It tends to be those with a 'secularizing' agenda of one kind or another, who wish to level down, and thus to neutralize, the influence of all faiths. For instance, if faiths can only influence legislation when they can act together, the impact may be significant but it will take place at the lowest common denominator and not too frequently. Again, if there is no acknowledged spiritual heritage, how will places of worship be provided in new housing areas, and for whom? The default position will then be to provide no places of worship. Religious education in schools will look more and more like a *smorgasbord* of interesting practices, ritual, feasts, etc. from different religious traditions rather than a serious evaluation of them from a committed standpoint. It will increasingly be unable to equip pupils to find a spiritual and moral vision by which to live. Instead, it will present them with the phenomenology of a number of religions without teaching them how to make any kind of informed choice.

In fact, as Lord Habgood has pointed out, there is no necessary contradiction between being a distinctively Christian country and a welcoming country.[25] The Judaeo-Christian tradition has a great deal to say about welcoming strangers and being just and generous towards them (Lev. 19:33; Is. 56; Rom. 12:13f. and *passim*). To acknowledge the Christian roots of

British society, for example, is not to deny others the opportunity of making their contribution. Indeed, to situate such contributions within an overall framework may be the means by which they are made possible. It is now generally admitted that there really is no 'neutral' point of view that can accommodate and adjudicate between different committed positions. The claims for such neutrality are made by what is itself a distinct philosophical position and many religious people feel that it may be the least welcoming of all.

It is certainly possible for Britain to be both a plural society and a society that acknowledges its Christian basis. Much hangs on the meaning of words and, contrary to opinion in some circles, they cannot be made to mean anything we choose. There is, for instance, a difference between 'plural' and 'pluralist'. It is undoubtedly the case that Britain, the USA and many other countries are 'plural' in the sense that there are people from many different religions, ethnic groups and political backgrounds living in them. Does that make them 'pluralist'? Not necessarily, unless by 'pluralism' we mean the sort of civic pluralism commended by Martin Marty, which involves not only permitting diversity of religious and ideological opinion in a nation, but also safeguarding it and encouraging different groups to make a contribution towards the development of national life, moral, spiritual and political.[26] As I understand it, Marty distinguishes this from the theological pluralism that regards all religions as variant expressions of a common spirituality directed towards an acknowledgment of both transcendence and immanence. The differences between religious traditions are, on this view, explained (or explained away) as arising mainly out of historical, cultural and linguistic differences.[27]

When it is said, therefore, that we live in a 'pluralist' society, what exactly is meant? Does it mean that we live in a diverse society? Such an assertion cannot be gainsaid. Does it mean that people's freedom of belief, of expression and of worship should be protected? Again, this is uncontroversial. It is quite a different matter, however, if it means that a nation does not distinguish between one tradition and another for its sources of law, government and ruling principles. In Britain, such a view flies in the face of our constitutional arrangements even if it informs much of what politicians and civic leaders do from day by day. In the United States, while there can be no single established Church, the nation's conscience continues to be fed by Christian belief, worship and practice.[28] It is that conscience, and the laws, political arrangements and liberties resulting from it, that can best serve the plurality that is the USA and not the *tabula rasa* beloved of certain kinds of liberal thinkers, politicians and even theologians. George Weigel, the American writer, likens this latter view to the giant cube built in the middle of Paris by the former French President François Mitterrand. Weigel calls it 'rational, angular, geometrically precise but essentially featureless' and contrasts it with the Gothic glories of Notre Dame with its 'vaulting and bosses, the gargoyles and flying buttresses, the nooks and crannies, the asymmetric and holy unsameness'. He asks which culture is better able to protect fundamental human freedoms – the culture that produces postmodern featurelessness or the one that has produced the movement to faith, hope and love.[29] It is a question we would do well to ask ourselves.

Just as confusion attends terms such as 'plural' and 'pluralistic', so also with compound words such as 'multi-faith' and 'inter-faith'. In some contexts these words are a straightforward description and if used correctly pose few, if any, problems. If it is said, for example, that Britain is a multi-faith society, meaning that people from a number of faiths live here, this is obvious and cannot be denied. If it is said, further, that public institutions such as hospitals and prisons should make multi-faith provision for their clients, there can be no objection, as long as this means providing access for their own faith leaders – whether these leaders are on the institution's staff or brought in from the wider community. If, however, it means giving over a dedicated or consecrated Christian chapel for multi-faith use or the undertaking of 'covenants' that prevent Christians and others from claiming distinctiveness for their faith, that is quite another matter.

Sometimes 'multi-faith rooms' are provided in public build-ings. If this stems from financial necessity or a lack of space, there can be little objection as long as the space does not become a multi-faith mishmash of bric-a-brac from the various traditions. It should, rather, be simple and unadorned so that the integrity of each person and group is respected. Groups that use the room can bring with them, and then take away again, whatever they need. In this way, the sensibilities of other users will not be offended. In a largely Christian environment, the best arrangement would still be a dedicated chapel and also some facilities for people of other faiths. Christians and others living in Muslim-majority countries would not dream of questioning the existence of a mosque within the boundaries of a public institution. They would be delighted, of course, if separate facilities were made available for them.[30]

The question of multi-faith worship arises more and more frequently these days. Political and civic authorities, community leaders, ordinary folk and, sometimes, even church leaders feel this is appropriate at times of celebration or of sorrow in national or local life. Such events are occasions for sharing solidarity, especially at times of crisis, or for affirming ministries of various kinds. Long ago, I wrote that multi-faith worship can never become part of the ordinary devotional and liturgical life of Christians since that is Christ-centred, which multi-faith worship cannot be.[31] As a woman who wrote to me recently said, 'God was mentioned but not Jesus.' That is the rub, or the stumbling block, if you like, because such events have often to be arranged around the minimum that is acceptable to all parties.

So what is possible, then? From time to time, people of different faiths and of none will ask Christians to pray *for* them or even *with* them.[32] As these are private and pastoral occasions, not only is there no harm in them, but they can also be important ways of bringing Christ's healing into the homes and lives of men, women and children who might otherwise remain unreached. On national days, civic authorities or embassies may wish to organize a 'function' where people of different faiths are asked to read from their scriptures and to offer a prayer. After the Bali bombings a few years ago, the Indonesian Embassy in London wanted to organize a memorial for those who had died. At the time, my advice to them was to ask people of different faiths to have a 'series' of memorials with others present, if they wished to be, as observers. Thus we had Christian (ecumenical),

Muslim, Hindu and Buddhist events following one another. Each had its own integrity and there was no compromise. When Pope John Paul II invited leaders of world faiths to Assisi, I understand that they came together in silence but each group had its own arrangements to pray for peace, if they wished to do so.[33] These so-called 'observances' are also about the idea that people of different faiths can bring out the riches of their own tradition in the presence of others. I have to say, however, that more and more often, these observances are becoming like unreconstructed multi-faith services.

In many cases, it is enough to have a distinctively Christian service to which people of other faiths are invited and where they are given seats of honour. Before the service begins, but preferably afterwards, they may be asked to bring a greeting or a thought. This is what we have done in Kent and south-east London and it seems to be appreciated on all sides.

I hope that the next coronation will remain a Christian event at which the sovereign is consecrated to Christian service in the context of the Eucharist and is told to defend the Catholic faith.[34] At such an event – which I hope will involve Christians of all traditions – people of other faiths and of none will be welcomed and honoured. Afterwards, there might be an occasion when they could bring their own good wishes to the sovereign, who would then want to say something to them. But let us not confuse the ancient coronation service with a well-meaning, but ultimately incoherent, mixing of various elements that are in fact immiscible. Sometimes, to my own embarrassment, I am asked whether the sovereign can be 'defender of faith' or 'of faiths' rather than of 'the faith'. The coronation service is crystal clear on this point: the King or Queen must uphold the historic, biblical and catholic faith – nothing less and nothing more. If 'defender of faith' or 'of faiths' means that he or she is to guard and maintain the possibility of faith and of freedom for people of different beliefs, then there can be no objection. Any claim, however, to uphold every faith is, of course, patently absurd as they contradict one another in important and even central matters.

The term 'inter-faith', as in 'inter-faith relations', can refer simply to how people of different faiths relate to one another in a community or nation or even globally. Similarly, 'inter-faith dialogue' can mean the very necessary discussion there has to be among people of different religious allegiances in order that they may understand one another's beliefs, exchange experiences and agree common principles for the building of community or to foster fundamental freedoms. Such uses of the term are uncontroversial. There is, however, a growing inter-faith 'industry', one of the aims of which is to minimize differences between the faiths on the grounds that this makes for greater social harmony. This is a very questionable assumption indeed. In fact, it may be that it is precisely a true understanding of difference that encourages people to work out a *modus vivendi*. My own experience of dialogue with Muslims, for instance, is that such dialogue has more integrity if distinctiveness is recognized from the outset. Fudging important issues and attempting a superficial and false harmonization gives a sense of unity that is untrue and, more seriously perhaps, prevents real differences from being acknowledged and discussed.

The term 'inter-faith' has also come to mean an approach to belief that sees the various historic faiths as variants of a *philosophia perennis*. The aim is then to discover the underlying faculty for believing and even an alleged common basis for all faiths. Some expositions of Indic religions profess sympathy for such a position, as may mystical tendencies in Islam and Christianity. Modern expositors of Vedanta, the final parts of the Hindu Scriptures, often hold that all faiths, *mutatis mutandis*, point towards the Absolute Reality (which philosophical Hinduism calls Brahman), where all differentiation is shown to be false.[35] Some Christian (or post-Christian?) theologians, such as John Hick, have advocated a 'Copernican revolution' in theology that would move Christian theology from 'Christocentrism' to a faith that is theocentric. All religions are then seen as different paths to the same divine reality, whose various aspects are revealed in different ways and to a different extent in each. Such a position denies, of course, any distinctiveness to the Christian faith beyond its historical and cultural expressions, and avowedly wishes to move away from a position that regards Jesus Christ as being at the centre of Christian concern.[36]

Sufism, or Islamic mysticism, is notoriously difficult to evaluate. How did it arise? What were the influences upon it? What is its position on questions of distinctiveness? Scholars such as R.C. Zaehner have distinguished between different kinds of Sufism. Sometimes, and at particular stages, it may manifest tendencies similar to nature mysticism. At other times, it may sound pantheistic, with God being seen in everything, and at yet others, it can be definitely monistic, not unlike Vedanta, with God understood as the sole reality. Both Zaehner and Allāma Iqbal have, however, also identified a kind of theistic Sufism in which the believer is united to the divine Beloved through a relationship of love but not of identity.[37] In the pantheistic or monist manifestations of Sufism, Sufis can and do sound like those who have moved to a post-religious phase of spiritual experience. As the doyen of Sufism, Jalāluddīn Rūmī puts it:

Na Tarsā na Yahūdam man na Gabram na
Musulmānam
Ba juz yā Hū ō ya-man Hū kasī dīgar namīdānam.

I am neither a Christian nor a Jew, not a Zoroastrian nor a Muslim.

I know none other than O He and O He who is![38]

Here the unity of mystical experience takes precedence over the formal doctrine and practices of particular religious traditions. Rūmi, of course, has more orthodox moments, as do many Sufis, but it is these aspects of his work that appeal to those involved in New Age type movements who are looking for human unity beyond 'dogma'.

Detailed study of the history of religions and the phenomenology of religion has shown that claims about all religions being but manifestations of one universal and fundamental spirituality are simply wrong. Religions arise from different visions of spiritual reality and of human significance and destiny. Their distinctiveness needs to be researched and respected, not abandoned in the search for some elusive oneness, which may exist only in the minds of certain kinds of people.

As for those Christian theologians who wish to move to theocentricity (as opposed to Christocentricity) because they feel this will bring different religious traditions into closer unity, they have been dealt with very effectively by Gavin D'Costa. In his devastating critique of John Hick's work, D'Costa points out that they succeed in building a universal system mainly by 'smuggling' back into their discourse specifically biblical and Christian ideas about God, love, the significance of humanity, etc. At the very least, it may be questioned whether all other faith traditions would acknowledge the importance of such ideas to the same extent if, indeed, at all.[39]

Similarly with Sufism, as we have seen, Zaehner and Iqbal show that pantheism, and experiences of oneness with nature, which lead to 'indifferentist' views of religious traditions, are 'immature' stages for Sufis and the attainment of maturity and what the Sufis call *baqā ba'd alfanā* (survival after annihilation) leads to a robust expression of orthodox theism as understood by Islam.

Just as the term 'multi-faith' should be restricted to the recognition of, and provision for, the existence of different faiths side by side, so also 'inter-faith' should be used only for relations among the different faiths and not be applied to some newly-emerging religion. These terms can be useful as adjectives but are both grammatically and theologically wrong when used as nouns.

We see, then, that Jesus is central to understanding the wellsprings of the fundamental values that are being universally recognized today as essential for a world order in which there is even a chance of justice, peace and compassion. Those who are called by his name and follow him know also that these values are transcended and transformed in him, enabling his followers to live by them so that they become rooted in their lives and help them to challenge and change the world.

Who is this person who stands at the centre of history and discloses the meaning and the destiny of the universe? Down the ages, billions of people have counted it their pride and joy to follow him. In his name, the world continues to be turned upside down. It is to this figure, of history but beyond it, from a people but greater than them, Lord of the Church but also of the world, that we now turn.

2

Who is Jesus?
The Unique and Universal Christ

No figure in history has been more studied, researched, commented upon and criticized than Jesus of Nazareth. Before he comes to his own arguments, Tom Wright, the Bishop of Durham, in his *Jesus and the Victory of God*, sets out some of the results of Jesus research and writing during the last century and a half or so. There are quests, new quests and first, second and third quests. There are scholars who are primarily interested in what Jesus said and others who are more concerned about what he did. There are those who regard him mainly as a teacher and those who see him as one who came to warn of the imminence of the arrival of God's reign. There is tension between those who are inclined to consider the theological significance of Jesus and those who want to take the history more seriously. Wright himself wishes to take history very seriously but also to put it at the service of the theological and practical task of the Church. The theological relevance of Jesus cannot be separated from the historical task of discovering his agenda, what others thought of him and what he thought of himself.[1]

Curiously enough, the historical approach has also been a leading concern of some liberation theologians in Latin America and elsewhere because a 'historical Jesus' is needed for authentic praxis. If our 'Jesus' is simply a ground for theological ideas, however sublime, or a provider of precepts and aphorisms, how does this help with the daily struggle of the oppressed and marginalized in confronting and converting those who oppress them? A Jesus is needed who himself struggles with evil, indeed, who is overcome by those forces that oppose his agenda of healing, freeing and including, and yet who is victorious at the very time that the powers of darkness seem most dominant. Theologians such as Jon Sobrino seem quite aware of the European and North American debates but their interest in the debates arises from their pastoral and missionary situation, which requires that history should not be bypassed but transformed.[2] Theologians from Korea also see the 'story of Jesus' as important because it helps them relate the gospel to the *han*, or the experience of suffering, of the Korean people.[3] Theologians from other parts of Asia similarly link Jesus' suffering with the suffering of their own people.

As one espousing a historical approach for the sake of the theological task, Wright gives us a clue to the rich historical resources that are now available. He finds the rehabilitation of Josephus congenial. Geza Vermes' pioneering work on the Jewishness of Jesus and on the Jewish background to his short life has made this aspect of Jesus studies almost *de rigueur*. The Qumran material and contemporary (or near-contemporary) apocalyptic literature cast a flood of light on first-century Palestine, on the world view of its inhabitants and on their expectations. In addition, there is Roman and other evidence.[4]

In spite of all of this rich material, our basic source of information about Jesus remains the New Testament and, in particular, the four Gospels. The latter are generally acknowledged as being a new kind of literature. It has long been denied that the Gospels are 'biography' and scholars have claimed that they are more like 'tracts for the times' to challenge people and to bring them to faith in the Christ who has been raised from the dead and is now the Lord of the universe. But against this, Richard Burridge and others have shown that the Gospels *are* biographies, though of a special, sacred kind.[5] They arose out of the Early Church and its need to understand more fully its own nature and mission, but they can, and do, provide us with more than sufficient material about Jesus' aims, the strategy he pursued in the fulfilment of those aims, the crucial events surrounding his suffering and death and his (growing?) understanding of himself and the work he had been called to do. The Gospels can be used, then, for information about Jesus, but critically, taking into account not only the mass of historical, literary and cultural evidence now available, but also the work of scholars over the last couple of centuries.

From the Gospels it seems clear that the mission of Jesus was focused on the renewal of Israel, on the fuller working out of the implications of returning from exile in Babylon and on the restoration of an acknowledgement of God's sovereignty. This last emphasis makes the imminence of the kingdom of God extremely important – the God of Israel is not some distant deity exercising tyrannical rule over the world and the people he has specially chosen to reveal his will. He is, rather, the God who is among his people, healing, restoring and preparing them through those whom he sent and then coming in his own person. There is a tension between God sending his prophets and, perhaps, even the Messiah, and God coming himself, a tension that is reflected in Jesus' own understanding of his work, as set out, for example, in the material peculiar to Luke, in the so-called Nazareth manifesto, and in the answer to the followers of John the Baptist, which is to be found in material common to Matthew and Luke (Lk. 4:14–28; Mt.11:2–19; Luke 7:18–35). In the first, Jesus, in the course of public teaching in the synagogue, applies to himself a passage originally about prophetic activity or about the Servant of God (Is. 61:1–2). The immediate result is apparent approbation among his listeners. It is only when he draws out the implications of his ministry that his hearers become enraged to the point of wanting to kill him. In the second case, Jesus refers the followers of John to another passage in the book of Isaiah, Isaiah 35:4–6, which is about the coming of God and the healing that results from it – once again applying it to himself. Is Jesus simply an agent of God (however exalted) or is he, in some way, the presence of God among his people? This question hangs over all of Jesus' activity, the response of his followers and the charges eventually levelled at him.

If Jesus' message was about the imminent arrival of God's kingdom, how this was being revealed in his own work and the need for his hearers to grasp it for themselves,[6] this immediately raises questions about what Jesus thought of himself. How were his words and his work related to his person? Who was he? What had he come to say and to do? Did he think of himself as unique in his person as well as his work and, whatever his commitment to the renewal of Israel as a people, did he see that there were universal implications in his vocation?

Omar Raageh's BBC television programme, *The Miracles of Jesus*, concentrates on a number of miracles that disclose to Jesus' disciples and to the vast crowds who followed him something of who Jesus thought he was. There is, for instance, the stilling of the storm: who could have such power over the elemental forces of the universe except Israel's God who had brought about an ordered creation out of a watery chaos? Then there is Jesus' repeated tendency to forgive people's sin, to include them and to set them right with God. This is exemplified in his treatment of the paralytic. He first deals with what is basically the matter with the man, that is, his alienation from God because of wrongdoing, and then heals him of his physical infirmity (Mk. 2:1–12 and parallels). This attitude is also shown in Jesus' habitual association with outcasts and sinners (e.g. Mt. 9:9–13) and, specifically, in the way he deals with Zacchaeus, the tax collector, when he explicitly announces the coming of salvation to him and his household, apparently completely bypassing the cultic role of priests, sacrifices and Temple (Lk. 19:1–10). He seems to be saying that all of the fragmentary and partial tokens of God's love and mercy towards sinners in the past are now focused and fulfilled in his person and work.

Raageh also believes that Jesus' exorcisms are a sign of his divine authority and of God's victory over the many and various forces of evil in the world. Raageh's testimony, as a believing Muslim, is particularly significant. He claims that the Qur'ān and Islamic tradition do not emphasize the miracles of Jesus precisely because they would lead to an assessment of him as divine. I believe, however, that he is mistaken in this view. The Qur'ān records classes of Jesus' miracles, such as those having to do with healing the sick, feeding his disciples and even raising the dead (3:49; 5:113–115, etc.) What it does say about these miracles is that they have occurred *b'idhni Allahi* (by

God's leave). In addition to the miracles recorded in the canonical Gospels, the Qur'ān also notes some of the miracles mentioned, for instance, in the infancy gospels, such as the bestowal of life on birds of clay by the breath of Jesus. In this connection, it is worth remembering that in Sufism and, therefore, in popular Islam, the breath of Jesus is associated with healing.[7]

It has often been noted that the Qur'ān has a singular view of Jesus: not only is he *nabī* (prophet) and *rasūl* (apostle), but he is also *kalima* (Word) and *rūh* (spirit) of God (2:136; 4:171; 19:30, etc.). He is born of a virgin, performs many miracles and is taken up in glory. Muslims believe that Q4:157 means that Jesus was not crucified but exalted by God to himself. His death, however, is mentioned in 19:33 and, arguably, in 3:55. To reconcile the two positions, it is often held that Jesus will return to earth and then die a natural death before the general resurrection. In this way, the Qur'ānic teaching both about his death and his resurrection can be fulfilled. The Qur'ān certainly teaches that prophets and even apostles, including Muhammad, can be killed (2:61,87; 3:144). So why is there such a reluctance to admit that Jesus could have been? Is there an implicit Christology in such a position? In any case, with evidence from extra-biblical sources such as Tacitus, Josephus and the Talmud, the crucifixion of Jesus has long been regarded a bedrock in history. Popular films, for instance *The Passion of the Christ*, have once again given it a credibility difficult to counter.

For centuries Christian apologists have asked what terms like 'word' and 'spirit' of God can mean, especially since Muslims use these words to describe Jesus. Any attempt, however, to build a high Christology on these terms, on the miracles or on what the Qur'ān has to say about the death, resurrection and exaltation of Jesus must reckon with the fact that some of the very passages that use these terms, or discuss the miracles, are also determinedly reductionist.[8]

In his important work, *The Muslim Jesus*, the Arab scholar Tarif Khalidi has shown the distinctiveness of Muslim views of Jesus. The Qur'ān is concerned mainly with arriving at a properly doctrinal view about him. The Hadith literature concentrates very much on Jesus as an eschatological figure whose return is to herald the last days, and then there are the Sufi related stories of his asceticism, piety and miracles. In all of this, Khalidi is quite clear that the Islamic Jesus and the 'Muslim gospel' are quite different from the Christian ones.[9]

There is, then, considerable Islamic material about Jesus from a number of points of view and from different periods, right up to modern times. There is also experience of Jesus among Muslims, which often takes the form of a vision or a dream followed by healing. Such experiences can be frequent in cultures where the supernatural is taken for granted and they can be life-changing.[10] It would be very interesting to hear how a Muslim such as Omar Raageh could bring together, and review critically, what he has learnt from the Christian tradition about Jesus and what his Muslim background has taught him. It may be that he will address this in the future.

Almost from the beginning, relations between Jews and Christians have been stormy. While early Christian mission benefited from the Jewish presence in many parts of the ancient world, the Acts of the Apostles also shows considerable tension and conflict.[11] The writings of the second-century Apologists and Jewish polemic show the ferocity of the debate.[12] The medieval *Toledoth Yeshu* (or *Story of Jesus*) preserves some early Jewish polemic about the circumstances surrounding the birth of Jesus, and the Talmud taught that Jesus was put to death because he had deceived the people.[13] The much remarked upon anti-Semitism of some early Fathers has to be set against the cursing of the *Mīnīm* (including Christians) in the so-called Eighteen Benedictions,[14] and the expulsion of Christians from the synagogues towards the end of the first century, exposing them to Roman persecution.[15]

When Christianity became the state religion in the Roman Empire, the codes of Theodosius and of Justinian systematized the prohibition on paganism and the penalties for heresy. They also instituted discrimination against the Jewish community (it is, indeed, ironic that these codes later became the templates for the codification of Shariah, which incorporated many of their features in its elaboration of the *dhimma* or the status of tolerated religious communities within the world of Islam).[16] Relations between Jews and Christians were no better within the Persian

Empire, the other great superpower of the time, as events during the persecution under Shapur II reveal.[17] This unhappy situation of polemic, persecution and conflict has continued down to our own times. It is only since the Holocaust, which was certainly inspired by the neo-pagan ideology of Nazism but to which Christian anti-Semitism, wittingly or unwittingly, contributed, that there has been a willingness for dialogue and a better relationship.[18] An aspect of the better relations that have been developing is the recovery of Jesus as a Palestinian Jew. This has allowed Jewish writers to evaluate Jesus in their own terms and it has enabled Christians, once again, to appreciate how the Jewishness of Jesus bears on questions of Christian origins. Since Geza Vermes' book, *Jesus the Jew: A Historian's Reading of the Gospels*, both Jewish and Gentile scholars have poured tremendous energy into this area. Such has been the success of this approach that it is now virtually impossible to disregard the Palestinian (and wider) Jewish background to the life and ministry of Jesus.

It is important, nevertheless, to remember that a common commitment to take seriously the Jewishness of Jesus does not exclude disagreement about the significance and claims of Jesus. Thus both Vermes and Cohn-Sherbok deny that Jesus is the Messiah expected by Israel while affirming that he was *hāsīd* (a pious Jew, Vermes) or a prophet of the Older Testament type (Cohn-Sherbok). Christian writers, on the other hand, may affirm the Jewishness of Jesus but still find room for his challenge to the different schools of contemporary Judaism and his particular consciousness of an intensely close relationship to God his Father, as well as his own view of what Messiahship entailed.[19]

There is certainly a theological debate to be had about messianic expectations in both Christianity and Judaism. Jews continue to expect the coming of the Messiah and of the messianic age that he brings, while Christians look for the parousia or the second coming of the Lord Jesus, and from the earliest times have prayed the Aramaic prayer *Maranatha* (1 Cor. 16:22). Is there a convergence here in that each side is expecting God to reveal his final purposes in the coming of the Messiah? The remaining difference would then be that for Christians the shape or form of this expectation has already been given in Jesus of Nazareth.

Given the Jewish sympathy for Jesus, which has just been discussed, how far can Jews within the integrity of their own faith see the marks of the coming messianic age in the figure of Jesus? Naturally, this is a question we cannot answer for them, but scholars such as Pinchas Lapide have pushed the debate further on towards a full scale re-evaluation of Jesus, whatever its results may be.[20]

The relation of Christianity to Judaism is unique. Not only was Jesus a Jew, but the apostles were also, as were the earliest churches. The receiving, reading and studying of the Hebrew Bible continues to have a huge and formative influence on the Church. New Testament research is making it more and more clear that Jesus was understood by the early churches in mainly Jewish categories of expectation and hope; the earliest assemblies of Christians drew on the synagogue for models of governance and of worship. Clearly there were differences, for example, in the role of women and in the way some elders, at least, had a specific profile in teaching and in the leading of worship. These differences cannot, however, negate the similarities.[21] As the Second Vatican Council's Declaration on the Relation of the Church to Non-Christian Religions, *Nostra Aetate*, puts it, the Church needs to understand the Jewish people in order to search the depths of its own mystery. It draws nourishment from the good olive tree on to which the wild olive branches of the Gentiles have been grafted (Rom. 11:17–24). In other words, if we are to have any hope of understanding something of Jesus and of the movement he initiated, we have to look to the Jewish people for information and inspiration.[22]

With both Judaism and Islam, Christianity has close historical and, whatever the differences, theological connections. Even on fundamental issues, we are in the same domain of belief in one God as creator of the universe, in the creation and destiny of human beings and in God's guidance so that human destiny can be nurtured and fulfilled. None of this is true of Hinduism where the whole topography changes with, on the one hand, the monism of the learned and, on the other hand, the vigorous polytheism of the masses. Estimates of the significance of human life and of its destiny are quite different, as are understandings of the world in which we live.

In spite of these huge differences of world view in both theology and anthropology, Jesus has an unexpected prominence here as well. It is true, of course, that the ancient Churches of India have borne witness to Christ for two thousand years. It is only, however, with the advent of the modern missionary movement of the last two hundred years or so that Jesus, his person, teachings and values have made a profound impact on Hindu society. Since then, Indian Christians have been attempting both to see the anticipations of Christ in Hinduism itself and also to show how these anticipations have been fulfilled in Jesus of Nazareth, who 'recapitulates' in himself all the authentic spiritual aspirations of human kind.[23] The doctrine of recapitulation or *anakephalaiōsis* is implied in Ephesians 1:10, where it is said that God's purposes are to bring all things to the fulfilment of their eternal destiny in Christ. This doctrine is then used and elaborated by St Irenaeus to indicate the totality of God's purposes for human redemption and their fulfilment in Christ.[24]

If Jesus came as fulfilment of the 'unknown Christ of Hinduism',[25] he came also as challenge to a Hindu society riddled with caste, with superstition and with the inhuman and cruel practice of suttee. It is in this context that evaluation of Christ by the major Hindu reformers and holy persons is to be seen. Raja Ram Mohan Roy seeks a renewal of Hindu society by appealing to the moral teaching of Jesus, and Mahatma Gandhi finds in the Sermon on the Mount resources for a doctrine of non-violent struggle. Both S.J. Samartha and M.M. Thomas have, in different ways, considered the question of Jesus within the Hindu framework.

There can be little doubt that the encounter with Jesus Christ has changed and continues to change Hindus and Hinduism in surprising and important ways. This has happened in many different respects and at different levels of influence. The reformers' criticism of caste, the emancipation and education of women and the tendency towards an ethical monotheism have all taken place under explicitly acknowledged Christian influence. As the great Indian nationalist leader Vinoba Bhave is said to have remarked at the time of the Pope's visit to Mumbai for the Eucharistic Congress, 'I, for myself, can say on behalf of the whole of Indian culture that Christ is acceptable to India . . .' But in what ways this happens varies from place to place and person to person.

There are those who have accepted Christ as their Saviour and Lord (and only him) who, nevertheless, want to continue being Hindu in the cultural and national sense. Distinguished people such as Kalicharan Banerjea and the evangelical leader Paul Sudhakar may fall into this category. Others, such as the well-known evangelist Sadhu Sundar Singh, would not go as far as that but their style of life, worship and patterns of evangelism are self-consciously Indian.

Samartha refers to those Hindus who respond to Christ but without any sense of an exclusive commitment. Depending on their spirituality, Christ is seen either as a *sadguru* (true spiritual leader) or as another *avatar* (or incarnation of God, such as Rama or Krishna from the Hindu pantheon). Those who are inclined towards an ethical interpretation of the significance of Jesus see him as a guru, while others, more interested in the supernatural aspects of his person and work, regard him as yet another incarnation of the Supreme Being. Then there are those who commit themselves to Christ, and to Christ alone, but within the cultural and even religious framework of Hinduism. Finally, there are those who are committed to Christ and to the Church but maintain a critical attitude to the form of the Church's life, its priorities and the methods of mission that it adopts.[26]

It is interesting to note that the key question in Hinduism has to do with the uniqueness of Jesus Christ as the Word made flesh whose suffering and dying for our sake has created a wholly new situation so that human beings can have open access to, and an intimate relationship with, the God who is the source of their being. As we have seen, many Hindus are willing to say that Jesus is *an* incarnation of God but would deny his uniqueness in this respect. Similarly, they would acknowledge value in his suffering and death but deny that this can atone for the sins of the whole world. His resurrection is spiritualized to mean the realization of the divine in him. Once again, such realization is not seen as unique but is, in principle, open to everyone.

Hindu attitudes to the uniqueness of Jesus are strongly reflected in New Age beliefs about him. This is not wholly surprising as many New Age movements have been directly or indirectly influenced by neo-Vedantist ideas in Hinduism. In any case, the endorsement of the *philosophia perennis* by leading modern Hindu thinkers and the explicit teaching that all religions are at base the same and point towards the same reality is congenial to New Age thinking since it allows the pick 'n' mix approach to spirituality that has come to characterize the postmodern west.[27]

This discussion about how others have seen Jesus began with Omar Raageh's view, as a Muslim, that somehow the miracles of Jesus reveal what Jesus thought of himself. So if we have seen how Muslims, Jews and Hindus think of Jesus, can we now return to what he himself thought about his work and his person?

The Sri Lankan scholar Vinoth Ramachandra has sought to build on the work of Ben Witherington III in emphasizing the role of the wisdom tradition in Jesus' understanding of himself. In his search for the excluded, the disreputable and the lost, Jesus presents himself, according to Ramachandra, as embodying Divine Wisdom. This would have had immediate resonances for Jesus' contemporaries, aware of Proverbs 9:1–6 and Wisdom 9:18. His association with tax collectors and sinners would be justified because many of those who had been given up for lost would be saved and be incorporated into the people of God and 'wisdom is vindicated by her deeds' (Mt. 11:16–19, NRSV). For Ramachandra, once Jesus' understanding of himself as the locus of Divine Wisdom is granted, this becomes an interpretive key to understanding some other, hitherto obscure, sayings of Jesus. He points, for example, to Jesus' invitation to those who are tired and burdened to take on his easy yoke and light burden, as evoking Wisdom's invitation in the book of Ecclesiasticus to accept her yoke (Mt. 11:28–30; cf. Ecclus. 51:23–30). In the same way, Jesus' reference to himself as 'greater than Solomon' (Mt. 12:42) must mean that he is presenting himself as the source of Solomon's wisdom – as Wisdom come in the flesh.[28]

Such an understanding of the centrality of Wisdom in the Bible and in the mission of Jesus finds echoes in feminist theological and biblical scholarship. Women scholars have for long been fascinated by the female form for Wisdom in both Hebrew and Greek thought (*hokma* and *sophia*). Nor is this merely a reliance on the grammar of those languages but on the fact that Wisdom is presented as a woman who is pure, beautiful and radiant (Wisdom 7) and who invites the most unlikely guests to her feast – the simple, foolish and immature – so that they may learn to be wise. These scholars are well aware of the importance of Wisdom in the early Church's understanding of Jesus. They are concerned also with how the female form of Wisdom affects our understanding of women as being in God's image and thus with their place in the Church and in the world.[29]

If Jesus understood himself in the light of Divine Wisdom, this has obvious implications in terms of his treatment of women and their response to him. Christology, as always, has ramifications for anthropology and, particularly, for an adequately Christian anthropology in which both men and women are recognized as being in God's image, with a common mission and with a similarity-in-difference, which requires that they bring different approaches to the fulfilment of this one mission. Redemption in Christ does away with the distinctions, oppression and subordinations that result from the Fall and subsequent human sinfulness. It restores true fellowship and mutuality but also recognizes a proper complementarity in the Church and in the world, even as both men and women address the same tasks (Gen. 1:26–31; 3:6–19; Gal. 3:27–29; Eph. 5:21f., etc.)

The significance of the Son of Man sayings in the Gospels has been the subject of an intensive debate: some have understood them to be about Jesus' understanding of his own person and work in terms of the heavenly figure who appears in the Aramaic section of the book of Daniel (7:13–14). Others have thought (on the basis of a reading of Luke 12:8f.) that when Jesus spoke about 'the Son of Man', he meant a heavenly, apocalyptic figure *other* than himself. Then there are those who claim that Jesus used the term simply as a means of self-designation and it was only the Early Church that traced this usage back to Daniel and invested it with divine significance.

As far as the Early Church is concerned, it should be noted that the use of the term 'the Son of Man' is extremely rare in the rest of the New Testament and if the Church had discovered a new significance for it, it is strange that it was not used more often. In patristic literature, again, it tends to stand for the humanity of Christ rather than his divinity.

Professor Charlie Moule has written that the term *the* Son of Man is most simply explained as the use of a symbol, at once historical and eschatological, from the book of Daniel. It is a symbol of God's suffering people who are, in the end, vindicated for their faithfulness. According to Moule, Jesus applies this symbol to himself as the initiator and representative of such an obedient people. It was Moule also who drew attention to the significance of the definite article in *ho huios tou anthrōpou* (the Son of Man) in the Gospel use of the term. This, for him, distinguishes it from the general use, which might also be taken to be self-referential in meaning. Moule's thesis has recently been supported by Andy Angel, who has shown that, linguistically speaking, it was possible to distinguish between a general and an emphatic use of the term in the Aramaic of Jesus' time, and that, moreover, the general use could be, and was, translated into Greek *without* the article. The use of the article by the evangelists, therefore, shows that they are reporting an emphatic use (*bar enāsha*) by Jesus and that in doing this he was understood to be referring to a particular Son of Man.[30]

Evidence from the use of language can be added to literary and historical evidence. Tom Wright makes the point extremely well when he points out that the issue is not so much what Daniel 7 might have meant originally as what it meant at about the time of Jesus. Here he is clear that it was read in a 'messianic' way by at least some Jews of the time. He cites Josephus to show that this was one passage that caused the Jewish revolt, and refers to evidence in the Pseudepigrapha to show that there was widespread use of Daniel 7 not only to speak of the hope of Israel, but also of the anointed king who was at the heart of it.[31]

Jesus, then, identifies himself with the figure in Daniel, who is a representative of God's people and who is given divine authority and rule. He sees the way to this, however, as lying through rejection, suffering and death. Daniel 7 itself speaks of the tribulations of the people of God and of their ultimate vindication, but Jesus, of course, also relates the suffering and vindication to another theme in the Bible, that of the Suffering Servant of God.

The last of the Servant Songs, Isaiah 52:13 – 53:12, has become an important *testimonium* for the Church in that it provides a detailed account of the humiliation, suffering, death and final vindication of the *'Ebed Yahweh* (Servant of God). Nowhere else do we find such a clear representation of expiatory suffering for the sins of people. In the Gospels, however, the clearest reference to an understanding of Jesus as the Servant of God is not taken from this passage but from Isaiah 42:1–4. In Matthew 12:18–21, the Isaiah 42 passage is used as a commentary on the work Jesus was already doing among the people, though it should not be forgotten that Matthew also relates this work to Isaiah 53:4: 'He took up our infirmities and carried our diseases' (8:17). It is interesting in this connection to note that it was Pentecostal preachers and teachers who drew attention to the dangers of spiritualizing Isaiah 53:4 by translating *holī* and *makōb* as grief and sorrow when the plain meaning is disease and pain. They pointed out that the latter was the sense in which the words were taken by Matthew. For the best of them, there was a relationship between seeing the suffering of the servant as being expiatory, that is, dealing with sin, and seeing it as restorative, dealing with the consequences of sin, including weakness and disease.[32]

The Early Church continued to refer to Jesus as the Servant (*pais*) of God who had been rejected, betrayed and killed by both the Jewish and Gentiles rulers but who had been glorified by God, and whose power to heal was to be seen in the Church (Acts 3:13; 4:27,30). Isaiah 53 finds echoes throughout the pages of the New Testament and has, indeed, been one of the main ways in which the Church down the ages has sought to understand the mystery of the suffering of Christ.

The notion that God's prophets are often rejected and have to suffer is deeply ingrained in the biblical tradition. Just before and at the time of Jesus there was a well-established expectation both that the righteous would suffer and that their suffering would have redemptive value for the people. It is in this context that Jesus' own understanding of himself as the Servant (*diakonos*) who would give his life as a ransom for many is to be understood (Mark 10:45).[33] This last verse is, of course, echoed in Matthew (20:28) and is related to the Lucan passage in the somewhat different setting of the Last Supper, where Jesus describes himself as *ho diakonōn*, this time not just referring to his coming suffering and death but to his servanthood being an example to the disciples (Lk. 22:27). The Johannine story of the foot-washing similarly brings out Jesus' understanding of himself as the Servant whose suffering brings redemption and is to be emulated by the disciples as they proclaim this redemption (Jn. 13:1–20).

The Servant Songs as a whole speak of the Servant as representing the people but not as simply being a reflection of them. The Servant represents them in the sense of what is called 'corporate personality', that is the idea that an individual may both represent and embody the group that he (or she) heads. Thus the *'Ebed Yahweh* stands for the calling and destiny of God's people but he also has a mission to them (cf. Is. 49:5) and a mission beyond them (Is. 42:1–4). The Servant suffers on behalf of his people and is put to death so that his grave is among the wicked and yet he lives to bring the benefits of his death to others (Is. 53:7–12). His redemptive significance, moreover, is not just for Israel but is shown to be of universal significance. The Servant is, in one sense, an ordinary, even despised, human being, but in another, he is the 'arm of the Lord'. What he accomplishes is well beyond the resources of even especially endowed mortals.

Muslims, of course, love to describe Jesus not only as a *rasūl* (messenger) of Allah and as *nabī* (prophet), but also as *'abd* (servant). This stands within the Hebrew and, indeed, Syrian Christian tradition for describing those who serve God. It should be clear, however, that the biblical use of this term, especially in relation to Jesus, is not at all reductionist but is, rather, to do with the accomplishing of God's purposes in the person of the Servant.

Sometimes poets get to the heart of the matter in a way that exegetes and theologians cannot. This is what Muhammad

Iqbal has to say regarding the Servant of God in his Persian *magnum opus* the *Jāvīd Nāmeh*:

> Lā-ila tigho dam-i-ō ʿabduhu
> Fāshtar khā'hī begu hū ʿabduhu

> 'Except God' is the sword and its edge is 'His Servant'.
> If you wish it clearer then say, 'He is his servant!'[34]

Iqbal, as a devout Muslim, is, of course, referring here to the Prophet of Islam and, indeed, there is much in Sufi and devotional Islam that would refer to him in this way. It should be noted, however, that it is extremely unlikely that the Prophet of the Muslims ever thought of himself in these terms and that remains the verdict of orthodox Islam.[35] Such language does, though, seem to echo a biblical view of God's Servant, who is the primary agent in bringing truth to humanity and in working out the divine will in this world. He is thus shown to be not only representative of the people, but also of God.

The task of the Servant is certainly prophetic: the far coasts wait for his teaching (or Torah) but the designation 'the Servant' also evokes the choice of Saul and of David as kings in Israel (1 Sam. 9:17; 16:12). This representative figure can also be regarded as royal and this means, therefore, that there are messianic expectations in the Servant passages in Isaiah. Isaiah 61:1–3 is sometimes regarded as the earliest interpretation of the Servant Songs. Even if the primary reference to anointing in Isaiah 61:1 is to prophetic anointing (cf. 1 Kgs. 19:16), there are royal overtones present here as well and the section can properly be regarded as messianic. It is difficult to see how Jesus can have failed to have been aware of this when he declares in the synagogue at Nazareth that this prophecy is being fulfilled in his person and work. Indeed, if with some liberation theologians, we regard his reference to this passage as a manifesto of his mission and ministry, it then illuminates not only his priorities, but also his understanding of his own person.[36] The evangelists, similarly, when they seek to understand Jesus in the light of the Servant Songs, will have been conscious of their messianic import (e.g. Mt. 12:17–21).

In spite of all of the above, it seems to be universally agreed that Jesus was reluctant to use the term Messiah for himself. This is often explained by pointing out that the contemporary expectations of such a figure were of a ruler who would bring about the political liberation of Israel and ensure its prosperity and good standing among the nations.[37] At the same time, by his *actions* and his *words* he claimed to be the promised Messiah in a way that had been purified of all accretions. Tom Wright has shown how the triumphal entry into Jerusalem and the cleansing of the Temple evoke strongly messianic passages in Zechariah (9:9–10; 14:21; cf. Is. 56:7 and Mk. 11:1–10,15–19; Mt. 21:1–17; Lk. 19:28–46; cf. Jn. 2:13–22).

The Johannine account, however, also reveals that Jesus was identifying himself with the true Temple. The cultic meal that he instituted at the Last Supper was intended to replace the sacrificial cults of the Temple. His cryptic sayings about the destruction of the Temple and its rebuilding would therefore be seen not only as sacrilegious, but also as blasphemous; in speaking of himself as the Temple that would be destroyed and rebuilt, he was claiming that he was the locus of God's presence in the way the Temple had been (1 Kgs. 8:10–11).[38]

There are the actions but there are also the words: parables, riddles and thinly-veiled allusions all point to a messianic view of who Jesus thought he was and what he had come to do. The parable of the tenants is richly evocative of a number of messianic themes. The servants of the household come to ask for the fruit that the vineyard of Israel should be producing. They are rejected, beaten and killed. Finally comes the Son, who is also rejected and killed, thus bringing a terrible judgement on the tenants in the vineyard, that is, the leaders of the people of Israel and all those who are complicit in their crime.

Tom Wright is, of course, entirely correct in asserting that the figure of the Messiah at the time of Jesus was a human figure who was anointed for great tasks and was not understood in a divine or even quasi-divine way, so that we must be careful not to read later Christology into the term Messiah or Christ as it occurs in the Gospels.[39] This is true but we must not forget that the Gospels come from the early Christian communities that gave rise to the rest of the New Testament, and in these communities the title *Christos* is certainly associated with the highest Christological reflection (e.g. Rom. 8; 9:5; Eph. 1; Col. 1:15–23; Heb.1:1–3).

When John's disciples arrive and ask, 'Are you the one who was to come, or should we expect someone else?'Jesus refers them to his 'speech-acts' or 'performative utterances': 'Go back and report to John what you hear and see: The blind receive sight, the lame walk, those who have leprosy are cured, the deaf hear, the dead are raised, and the good news is preached to the poor' (Mt. 11:2–6; cf. Lk. 7:18–22). The interesting point about this incident is, of course, the fact that Jesus is referring here directly to Isaiah 35, which is about the coming of *God* to save his people.[40] Already in the Older Testament, the Messiah, as the descendant of David, is closely associated with divine rule (Ezek. 34:23–24; Ps. 89:3–4). Wright himself mentions Psalm 45, where the king shares the throne with Yahweh, and the letter to the Hebrews adds Psalms 2 and 110 to this testimony.

The cumulative effect of all this is to lead us to acknowledge that Jesus was reluctant to make too much direct use of the term 'Messiah' with reference to himself, both because of the expectations that had clustered around it and also because contemporary understandings did not bring out the full significance of the ascription. By word and action, however, he indicated all that it might mean. When faced with Simon Peter's confession, he does not refuse the title but goes on to speak of his approaching suffering as the proper context for this kind of messiahship (Mk. 8:27–38 and parallels). Again, at the time of his trial, when answering a direct and solemn question from the High Priest, Jesus' words, however they are understood, have the effect of admitting openly what he has so far, in public, at any rate, only alluded to in his words and in his acts (Mk. 14:60–62 and parallels). His understanding of the term, though, is peculiarly his own or, rather, it is his own but profoundly informed by the Hebrew Bible's teaching on the Son of Man, the Servant of Yahweh and the anointed King of David's line. The canonical Gospels and the other writings of the New Testament bear witness to this understanding that Jesus had of his own person and work.

The extent of the diversity in New Testament estimates of Jesus remains a matter of debate. But whether there is a single kerygma or a number of related kerygmata, a certain unity on the significance of Jesus for the Church and for the world can also be detected and it is this that gives rise to the 'rule of the faith'.[41] The emerging 'rule of faith' and the canonical books of the New Testament have a mutuality about them. As the late Professor Geoffrey Lampe used to say, the Scriptures determined the rule of faith and the rule of faith enabled the Church to recognize the authenticity of particular writings as Scripture.

Further reflection on the unity of the scriptural witness and the rule of faith, as well as the need to combat radical departures from the consensus, led, in due course, to the formulation of the so-called catholic creeds: the Apostles' Creed arising out of the confession of faith made at baptism and the Niceno-Constantinopolitan Creed out of councils of Church leaders convened precisely to consider and to oppose departures from the teaching that the Church had received, reflected upon and sought to transmit across the cultures and down the ages.[42]

Such departures seem to have occurred in three main ways: as the result of attempts to reduce Jesus to being 'a mere man'; or to show that he could not have been really human at all; or, thirdly, to reduce his memory to words or to the performance of (outlandish) miracles. We have Epiphanius' testimony about the Ebionites that, among other things, they believed Jesus to have been a created being, born in the ordinary way, who had nevertheless been adopted as the Son of God and exalted even above the archangels. In case anyone should have the idea that these Ebionites represented a kind of primitive Jewish Christianity that later Hellenization had corrupted, Epiphanius also points out that they were vegetarians and much of their polemic was reserved for the Jewish system of sacrifices.[43]

There are, then, a veritable plethora of Gnostic 'gospels', the purpose of which seems to have been to reduce Jesus to an oracle, a propounder of 'wisdom sayings', who imparted special knowledge to the hearers and readers who could then be saved from a material, fallen and evil creation. Even advocates of the Gospel of Thomas' early origins have to admit its disjointed nature, its Gnostic interests and its lack of interest in narrative, especially in the account of the passion, death and resurrection of Jesus Christ. This is sometimes explained by claiming that

Thomas is no different here from the other 'sayings sources' on which the canonical evangelists have drawn.[44] Such sources are, of course, hypothetical and we cannot be certain about the extent of what was contained in them. They do, however, cohere with the narrative patterns of the canonical evangelists and with the testimony of the Early Church regarding Jesus. Thomas and the other 'gospels' of this genre, by contrast, seem miles removed from the biblical world view, thought forms and *sitz im leben* of the canonical Gospels.

Koester claims, in this connection, that the terms 'heretical' or 'orthodox' are meaningless when considering the early gospel traditions and writings, whether canonical or not. Such a claim cannot be sustained, however, when the nature of these writings is examined. We then have to agree with the judgement of M.R. James that the number of books that are not in our canon but could have been included is very small indeed. He mentions the Epistle of Barnabas, the Shepherd of Hermas and 1 and 2 Clement. Even regarding these, he is deeply thankful that in the end they were not included. As for the rest, his judgement is that they were never read in the context of public worship and in congregations that were in communion with the 'generality' of other catholic congregations but belonged, rather, to adherents of certain teachers whose doctrines differed from catholic Christianity in fundamental ways.[45]

If Thomas is an example of the *logia* type of gospel, the infancy gospels make the child Jesus largely a worker of miracles and a somewhat petulant one at that. We have seen already that while some of the miracles of Jesus related in the Qur'ān seem of canonical origin, others, such as making birds of clay and breathing life into them, come from infancy gospels such as that of Thomas (different from the one above) or the Arabic gospel of the infancy. All of this literature, while it overlaps with, borrows from and has superficial similarities with the New Testament, has to be read to appreciate its distance and difference from the New Testament.

The rootedness of the New Testament documents in the first century AD, their relationship to the contexts they claim to describe, the agreement of the early Fathers with their witness and the emergence of creedal orthodoxy in their vindication, all give us confidence in the Scriptures and in what they teach about Jesus. Such teaching is not, of course, a dead letter: rather, it is maintained and sustained in the Church's living tradition, which seeks to keep the Church faithful to the apostolic testimony it has received and which is so richly confirmed in so many ways.

We have seen, then, how the Scriptures point to Jesus, how he himself understood them in relation to his person and how the Church has seen them as fulfilled in him. It is impossible, of course, to separate the person of Jesus from his work and it is to this that we now turn.

3

What Does Jesus Do?
The Unique and Universal Work

We experience a world that is fractured. Our own lives have a brokenness about them and our communities are divided, socially, economically and politically. Is the postmodern age unique in its sense of alienation and estrangement? It is certainly true that we have available a particular kind of vocabulary. From the time of Hegel, humanity's condition has been analysed in terms of conflict with nature, with others and, indeed, with the source of our very being. Karl Marx famously saw human alienation in terms of the labourer's relationship to the results of work, the product, which does not belong to the worker but to the employer. The 'commodification' of labour, moreover, brings about the division of labour, which now alienates the worker not only from the product, but also from other workers. The various schools of psychoanalysis have revealed the inner conflict that exists within the human personality, not least the war between the spiritual and the sensual, while both art and literature reveal themes of loneliness, the collapse of the community and the ubiquity of consumerism.

For Hegel, the cure of alienation is largely intellectual. Human beings need to resolve the contradictions that they encounter by thinking dialectically so that thesis and antithesis may be resolved into a hitherto unforeseen synthesis. Psychoanalysis seems to address states of alienation through approaches that encourage recognition of the reasons for the inner cleavage, integrative discipline for the personality and the reconciliation of the elements at war within the self. For Marx, the solution was, of course, proletarian revolution, which would end the exploitation of the worker by the capitalist and restore the individual or collective ownership of the product by the workers. However inadequate or mistaken these analyses of the human condition, we must recognize important connections with the Christian tradition: the human demand for an ordered, just and compassionate world, the need to be at peace with oneself and to live in a society where the wealth of one does not depend on the poverty of another.

Dr F.W. Dillistone, in his hugely imaginative work on the atonement, is aware that many of the themes of alienation, estrangement and disruption that seem to characterize modern and postmodern thought were in fact known in the ancient world. There is widespread recognition that somehow there has been a disruption in the primal harmony of the universe. Such disruption is evident in the conflict within nature 'red in tooth and claw', or it can been seen in the disturbance of social structures caused both by individual assertions of independence and by groups that for one reason or another have become restive.

Alongside such perceptions of disruption, different cultures and their accompanying religious traditions have instituted customs and rituals to restore that universal harmony. This 'nostalgia for paradise' is embodied in forms of sacrifice that seek to participate in that primeval and eternal sacrifice that brought the universe into being, keeps it in existence and renews it in its fertility and fruitfulness. Dillistone considers the three ancient cultures of Egypt, India and China as examples.[1] Sacrifices could be, of course, of animals, bullocks, rams and boars, as in the Chinese system, or of grain, firstfruits or libations of wine or oil. Animal sacrifice, in particular, enabled human beings to come to terms with what they most feared – blood, violence and death. The animal was offered to secure the well-being of the offerer and the wholeness of society.

When we come to the Bible's view of creation, its disruption and God's plan for its rescue and fulfilment, we enter another world altogether. To be sure, ancient oriental myths are in the background and some of the imagery and language is in common use. What is most noticeable, however, is that the mythological elements have been purified and distilled away so that we are left either with doctrine or with narrative that is very far from 'abstruse wonderfulness'.[2] They are, in fact, about the working out of God's purposes in creation, through the Fall, the calling of Abraham and the vocation of Israel, her faithful response or, indeed, her rebellion, exile and return. Most importantly of all, they are about God.

There have been many attempts to make the sacrificial system in Israel fit the renewal and fertility themes of sacrifice in the surrounding cultures of the Middle East but to no avail. In Israel, sacrifice seems mainly to have been concerned with the celebration of Yahweh's great acts of deliverance, or else it was expiatory. The celebration of the Passover, as an example of the former, was certainly a remembering, and a making effective in the present, of Yahweh's liberation of Israel from slavery and his continuing protection of them. It was also, however, a communion meal, which brought the members of each family, and the people as a whole, together in a common celebration. The expiatory kinds of sacrifice are denoted by a number of expressions in the Hebrew Bible such as *zebah*, *ashām* and *hattā't*. The last two stand for the offences they expiate while the first refers to that which is slain. The three terms can be used interchangeably but *ashām* better designates sins against God and neighbour where restitution can be made.

Yom Kippur is the great day of fasting, repentance and atonement when the themes of repentance and of forgiveness are fully to the fore. The very term *kippur* is related to the Arabic *kafara*, which means to cover or to hide, and to *kaffāra*, which to this day means atonement or expiation. In modern-day Judaism, the sacrifices prescribed for the Temple have been replaced by prayer, charity and food offerings but they still retain the element of substitution that was so integral to the sacrificial systems.[3]

The former Chief Rabbi, Lord Jakobovits, has pointed out the ambivalence that there is in Judaism in connection with sacrifice. On the one hand, it is at the very centre of the cult, which is unimaginable without it, but on the other hand, there is severe criticism of an over-reliance on the mechanical observance of the ritual without a change of heart and the intention to honour God with heart and mind.[4] In his essay, the Chief Rabbi points out that a critique of mechanical views of sacrifice is found in both the historical and the prophetic books, nay, it is found in the Torah itself. Having referred to 1 Samuel (15:22; cf. 7:17; 10:8; 16:2), the Chief Rabbi continues with a remarkable exposition of sacrifice in the prophetic books. He starts with Hosea, to whom he refers as 'the first literary prophet' and Hosea's preaching that God desires steadfast love and not sacrifice, the knowledge of God, rather than burnt offerings (6:6). He then goes on to Isaiah (1:10–17), to Jeremiah (7:21–23; cf. 17:26) and to the Psalms: 'The sacrifice acceptable to God is a broken spirit; a broken and contrite heart, O God, you will not despise' (51:17, NRSV). He points out that the writing prophets and the psalmist are not wanting to do away with the idea of sacrifice altogether but to put it in a proper perspective, which has to do with self-sacrifice, with a willingness to put God before our own narrow self-interest.

As the Chief Rabbi realizes, it is quite possible to be simply revolted by the sacrificial cult and turn away from it, perhaps to more contemplative and meditative forms of spirituality. Many people, particularly Christians, see the sacrificial system as just vain ritual, but should we have a more positive view of it? It certainly manifests a deep yearning for the restoration of a broken relationship, the healing of a great disruption, as, indeed, do the other sacrificial systems of the ancient world. But can we turn from the 'psycho-religious drama' it undoubtedly is, from the human perspective to the divine? If from the human side, the sacrificial system can be seen as anticipation, can it, from the divine side, be seen as promise? And if it is seen as promise, what is the fulfilment? Can we be content with a picture of the traditional sacrifices being restored in the messianic age, this time perhaps being extended to 'all peoples' (Is. 56:3–8) or, in the light of the prophetic critique, does the notion of sacrifice have to be radically transcended?

Dr Dillistone has shown how in many cultures there is an apprehension that sacrifice, if it is to be effective on a cosmic and universal scale, must itself be the sacrifice of one who is the source and ground of the universe's being, who can be representative, therefore, and inclusive. From the perspective of Jewish belief and practice, there is increasing recognition that human suffering, for example of the prophets, can and does contribute towards the fulfilment of the divine will (1 Kgs. 19:9–18; Jer. 26; Zech. 1:4–6, etc.). In the book of Wisdom, similarly, the righteous who suffer will be vindicated by God because of their trust in him (3:1–9). In both the Maccabean literature and in Qumran, the suffering and martyrdom of representative Jews is increasingly taken to be not only exemplary, but also as somehow redemptive for the whole people.[5]

We have seen already that in both the theme of the Son of Man and that of the Suffering Servant of God, these representative figures recapitulate in themselves the sufferings of God's people as well as their vindication by God. How sacrifice relates to obedience and how such obedience can be of salvific value to others is brought to a head by the first part of Psalm 40:

> Sacrifice and offering you do not desire,
> but you have given me an open ear.
> Burnt-offering and sin-offering
> you have not required.
> Then I said, 'Here I am;
> in the scroll of the book it is written of me.
> I delight to do your will, O my God;
> your law is within my heart.' (Psalm 40:6–8, NRSV)

Here the sacrificial victim is not an animal but a representative human figure whose obedience leads to communal deliverance.[6] It is no wonder that the writer of the letter to the Hebrews seizes upon this passage in its Septuagintal version with its more messianic overtones. In his commentary on these verses, the writer encapsulates the entire purpose of the sacrificial system, and also sees in the coming of Jesus the fulfilment of the hope for a representative figure who, by his work of suffering for the people, would be vindicated by God. By his freely-willed obedience, the incarnate Christ offers up all of himself as a final, unrepeatable and unique sacrifice to God.[7] As so often in the

Bible, the speculation, myths and wistful longings of humanity are brought to the bar of a historical event, a person in whom God is himself acting in a saving and sacrificial way. Here vanity is cleared away, speculation clarified and longing fulfilled.

The person of Jesus is understood through his work and this is focused in his suffering, death and resurrection. We have seen how, at times of disclosure for his disciples on who he was, Jesus refers them to his coming suffering and death. When Peter recognizes him as the Messiah, Jesus immediately goes on to talk about his rejection by the elders and leaders of the people (Mk. 8:27–31 and parallels). Peter is rebuked for attempting to distract Jesus from his vocation and Jesus declares his mission to call others also to walk the same path and to bear the same load (Mk.8:32–38). When James and John make their request about eminence in the kingdom, they are admonished and pointed to the way of service that is being opened up by Jesus' own self-giving sacrifice (Mk. 10: 35–45 and parallels).

We have seen how in Jesus' teaching this theme is central to his understanding of what he has come to do. It is impossible to take him seriously as Teacher and to neglect this aspect of what he believed about himself. In a telling passage, St Matthew connects the healing ministry of Jesus with the work of the Suffering Servant in Isaiah: 'He took up our infirmities and carried our diseases' (Mt. 8:17; Is. 53:4). Some scholars have seen this as a 'discrepancy' in that Matthew has applied a text about the atoning death of the Servant to Jesus' ministry of healing. D.A. Carson is surely right, however, in maintaining that Jesus' healing work arises from, and is made effective by, his atoning death. Illness is one of the consequences of the Fall and through his atoning death Christ has dealt with the consequences of the first sin and of all the following sins.[8] The cross is the basis and the source of healing, spiritual, social, psychological and physical, and should always be at the centre of the Church's ministry of healing.

In his highly suggestive book *Knowing Jesus*, James Allison writes of Jesus' awareness of his approaching fate as 'the intelligence of the victim'. Jesus understood his task as being about the setting free of all who were victims of a corrupt and selfish order where the weak were made scapegoats for the sins of the powerful and where their exclusion served to consolidate the society of oppressors. In this work of liberation, however, Jesus himself becomes a victim, is expelled and killed, thus leaving the oppressors as the apparent victors. Jesus knew that an oppressive world order would deal with the liberator in this way. Nevertheless, he did not flinch from what he had to do and God, in his wisdom and power, made the expelled and murdered victim the source of new life, of reconciliation and of peace, even for his murderers.

This new life is the basis of a new community, a new way of being human, which is open to all. Members of such a community live not by the old ways of victimizing others but by the 'law of Christ' (Gal. 6:2). Those who wish to be part of this 'grand inclusion' must accept the story of God's rescue of victims from the Exodus to Jesus and live in accordance with God's revealed plan for an inclusive and redeemed community. Such a community is 'over and against' whatever stunts human friendship with God and love of one another. It is *against* every thing that diminishes us and *for* all that enables us to live fully and abundantly.[9]

The cross of Christ, if it is what Christians believe it to be, must be seen as the most significant event in the history of creation. It is no less than the beginning again of a creation wrecked by human wrongdoing. God the creator begins anew the work of creation and of renewal, promised, to be sure, in the calling of Abraham and the story of Israel but repeatedly frustrated by human wilfulness, wrongdoing and obstinacy. The resurrection of Jesus is the firstfruits and the guarantee of the efficacy of this work (1 Cor. 15:20; cf. 2 Cor. 1:22; 5:5), which leads to a new heaven and a new earth. It both completes and continues that restoration of wholeness that is God's will for us. Countless individuals, families, peoples and nations are healed by it, saved through it and renewed because of it.

It is true, of course, that the cross is the culmination and climax of the whole of Jesus' life seen as 'at-one-ing'. His life of complete dedication to God's purposes is what opens up for us, once again, the way to God the Father. He did for us what we would not and could not do. It is as we stand with him, in him and by him that we too are found to be acceptable to God, reconciled to him and empowered by the Spirit to live as Jesus lived – with the whole of our lives a constant and pleasing offering (Rom. 12:1–2; Heb. 13:15).

Indeed, there are subjective responses to the cross of Christ. People are moved by the suffering of the innocent Jesus. Artists explore and respond to different aspects of the crucifixion. At the millennial *Seeing Salvation* exhibition at the National Gallery in London, themes drawing upon the sacrifice of Jesus were among those that were most popular with visitors. Composers and musicians, too, and poets down the ages and in every language, have attempted to express human feelings about the cross.[10] Jesus is seen, moreover, as an (perhaps *the*) exemplar for those who endure suffering and death for God's sake.

The roots of such views are in the Gospels themselves where Jesus, after predicting his own approaching passion, tells his followers to take up their crosses and follow him (Mk. 8: 31ff. and parallels). And this is how the cross was understood by the earliest disciples and in the Early Church. St Paul wants to share (*koinōnia*) in the sufferings of Christ (Phil. 3:10) and for the sake of the Church to be completing in himself whatever he has not experienced of this suffering (Col. 1:24). Ignatius also, on the way to martyrdom, wants to be an 'imitator of the passion of my God' (Rom. 6:3). The account of Polycarp's martyrdom, similarly, has him speak of sharing, with the other martyrs, in the cup of Christ (14:2).[11] It is the same today: many of those suffering persecution because of the name of Christ identify strongly with his sufferings while at the same time affirming the uniqueness of Christ's death as, indeed, did the earliest witnesses. It should also be remembered that Jesus is 'exemplar' in another sense in that by his suffering and death he manifests the extent of God's sacrificial love for his creatures and his desire to save them and to renew his creation. It is this prior love that evokes a loving and imitative response from us as we turn towards it and are healed by it.

Sufi devotion to Jesus is well known and well remarked but it concentrates on Jesus' powers of healing, his peacefulness, his utter devotion to God and his awareness of one-ness with God. There are numerous references to Jesus in Sufi writings and they have been thoroughly identified and commented upon.[12]

Surprisingly, however, there is also some mention of the cross, though it is not always clear whether it is the cross of Jesus that is meant or the Sufi martyr Mansūr Al-Hallāj's execution by the authorities for blasphemy. Tarif Khalidi, in his book *The Muslim Jesus*, refers to allusions to the cross in Muslim stories about Jesus but on examination they are vague and ambiguous.[13] Both Bishop Hassan and Bishop Cragg draw our attention to the famous verses in Rūmī:

> By love the cross becomes a throne
> By love the Knight his lowly mount
> By it the King becomes a slave
> And the dead raised to life anew.[14]

Once again, there are tantalizing glimpses of what might be meant here about incarnation and atonement but there is no proof.[15]

Already the poet Sana'ī (d. 1150) had seen that one must crucify self as Jesus did to know what obedience to God means. The clearest statement, however, about the cross is from Rūmī's thirteenth-century contemporary, Rukn al-Din Awhadī, who writes in detail about suffering for God's sake and Jesus as the embodiment of it:

> On the day when Jesus went to his task,
> And set himself upon the cross
> He said, if there is anyone present here,
> This is sufficient proof of love.
> Whoever turns his face to God,
> Must press the back against the cross,
> Until the body has been tied to the gallows
> The soul cannot ride to the heavens.[16]

This is a clearly exemplarist view in truly Abelardian style because it speaks of the cross as at once a demonstration of love and something to be emulated by the devout.[17]

The most we can say, then, of Sufism is that if the cross is mentioned at all, it is in an allusive way. We cannot be certain that in every case the reference is to Jesus or that when it is the emphasis is on Jesus' obedience and the need for us to follow in his footsteps. We need also to relate such references to the general Islamic teaching in this area, on which we have already commented.

Whatever we think or feel about subjective views of the atonement, it is clear that they cannot stand alone. If the cross is the world-changing event that Christians have always believed it to be, then there must be more to it than demonstration and response. In other words, we need robustly objective views of the atonement as well as subjective ones. Such views need to focus on the *transaction* that occurred on the cross. They must relate to a properly biblical anthropology, which affirms that human beings have indeed been made in God's image and likeness but that their waywardness, rebellion and obstinacy in wrongdoing have not only obscured and damaged the image of God in them and frustrated God's purpose for them, but have also fractured their relationship with the source of their being and thus cut themselves off from all that sustains wholesome living.

This situation, moreover, is endemic so that it cannot be dealt with by the human race, which has neither the will nor the means to deal with its profound alienation from its creator. On the one hand, each one of us is caught in the web of corporate sinfulness so that we cannot, of ourselves, break free. On the other, our wills are so enslaved to the world, the flesh and the devil that we cannot will even the good we know we ought to do. We need rescue from the situation in which we find ourselves. According to the Bible, however, the Creator is also Redeemer and the gospel in both the Older and the New Testament is about how God himself is to provide a way back for human beings.

This good news tells us that God has sent his Son, his eternal Word and creative Wisdom, in human form so that he might bring about reconciliation between God and ourselves. He does this not as an alien mediator but by radical identification with our humanity and also by profound newness. He stands in our place and does what we cannot and will not do. His whole life of God-centredness, of doing his Father's will, of utter dedication and obedience, is to be seen as the inauguration of a renewed humanity. As we have seen, the cross is the climax and fulfilment of this extra-ordinary atonement. By it the wrath of God, and its accompanying retribution, is averted from our personal and corporate wrongdoing. As our substitute, Christ offers up a pleasing sacrifice to the Father and turns away the penalty for sin due to us. As our representative, he stands for the whole of humanity and the scope of his atonement must be seen to extend to the whole.

There has been much debate about the extent of the atonement. Most Christians believe that Christ died for everyone and so that its extent is universal. Of these, the vast majority would also hold that while the atonement is universal in extent, in its saving effect it is limited to those who respond in some way with faith, love and obedience. There are others, however, who believe that Christ died only for the elect and thus the atonement is limited or particular in its scope.[18] They appeal for support to passages such as Matthew 1:21; 20:28, Mark 10:45 and John 17:9. They are also aware, however, of passages with a 'universal' dimension, such as John 3:16; Romans 5:18; 1 Timothy 4:10; Titus 2:11 and 1 John 2:2. These are explained as referring to all sorts, classes and groups of people in the world (*'from* every tribe and language and people and nation', Revelation 5:9) rather than to the whole of humanity. Personally, I incline to the modified universal approach that Christ died for all but that the fruits of his atonement have to be appropriated by faith, which is also, of course, God's gift to us and which needs to be received with humble thankfulness. However, even if a particularist view is taken, this should not in any way compromise Christ's representative humanity, especially in relation to his atoning work: redemption is, indeed, a new creation (2 Cor. 5:17).

The cross and the resurrection of Jesus from the dead, however continuous with the story of Israel, are also the beginnings of a new humanity now once again conforming to God's purposes. Nor can they be limited to humanity alone if it is God's plan to bring together or recapitulate in Christ 'all things in heaven and on earth' (Eph. 1:10). The whole of creation is promised renewal by Jesus' suffering and its vindication by God (Rom. 8; Rev. 21:1–7; 22:1–5). In this sense, redemption is really re-creation. It is restoring what has gone wrong and has led to frustration, violence and decay. It has universal dimensions, which extend beyond the Church and even humanity, however understood. Every aspect of the world is engaged, both the living world – the complex eco-system, which we call Earth and which makes life possible and viable – and the vastness of the universe itself.

A proper doctrine of creation tells us something of the nature and purpose of the universe and everything in it. It is, however, the 'lifting up' of Jesus (Jn. 12: 32), that is, his crucifixion, resurrection, ascension and glorification, which rescues creation from the 'futility' to which it has been subjected and gives us a glimpse of how God is renewing and transforming it. As St Paul reminds us, the resurrection of Jesus is but the firstfruits of a new creation (1 Cor. 15:20–29), the beginning of the fulfilment of God's purpose for his world, which will come to fruition when Christ appears in glory. We will then understand fully the transformation he has wrought. Our concern, then, for the world and for our fellow human beings is not simply rooted in our view of creation, of how things *are*, but in the resurrection, of how things *ought to be*. Moral insights, decisions and stances will then spring from a due appreciation of the implications of the cross and resurrection for humanity and for the universe as a whole.[19]

The universal implications of the cross remind us of the so-called 'classic' idea of atonement: the central point here is that in the conflict between God's will and those elements of his creation that resist his will, Christ, through his cross, has defeated the devil and all his works, winning a decisive victory and, among other things, liberating us from bondage to sin and death. In the *De Incarnatione* of St Athanasius, Christ dies 'in place of all' but in doing this he also wins a mighty victory for death cannot hold him. The benefits of his victory are available for those who put their trust in him: they are set free from the fear of death because they know they are to obtain the resurrection. This patristic idea, itself rooted in the New Testament (1 Cor. 15:54–57; 1 Jn. 5:4), was powerfully revived by Martin Luther. The victory has already been won and Christians enjoy the fruits of this now but also have the sure and certain hope that the effects of this victory continue to be extended until God is, indeed, all in all.

It was this sense of being on the winning side that gave Luther's theology such vigour. In recent times, the Swedish theologian Gustaf Aulén has argued powerfully for a renewal of this classic view. According to Aulén, Christ fights against and triumphs over evil. In Christ, God is defeating evil and reconciling the world to himself (2 Cor. 5:19). There is here a sense of action on God's part, which brings about a real and profound change in the way things actually are. Aulén is well aware of patristic and medieval crudities and absurdities that have surrounded this view of atonement: for example, Christ was described as the worm on the hook that finally caught Satan, and the cross as a bargain between God and the devil in which Christ was exchanged for sinners bound for hell. The devil thought he was getting a good bargain until he discovered that hell could not hold Jesus, who triumphed over it (cf. Acts 2:24). Aulén is nevertheless concerned to uphold the sovereignty of God in the defeat of the devil on the cross and in God's reconciling work in Christ.[20]

When we see Christ's work as substitutionary, representational and victorious, we are seeing the atonement in objective terms as an event that has made a difference. As our representative, he undoes the disorder of our old humanity and recreates in himself a humanity once again conformed to the divine will. By faith and through baptism we are incorporated into this new humanity. As our substitute, Christ offers his obedience in place of our disobedience, turning away God's wrath and reconciling us to him. As victor, he assures us of the triumph of the good and of our own destiny.

The cross is certainly declarative of God's love for us but this is no impotent affection that is unable to deliver us from our plight. It is a powerful, sacrificial and effective love, which is sufficient for our salvation. Again, the cross evokes a response of love and sacrifice in us but that is because we have been delivered from bondage and enabled to make this response. To use traditional language, because of the cross, the righteousness of Christ is imputed to us so that we stand before God clothed with Christ (Rom. 13:14; Gal. 3:27) and thus acceptable to him. But the grace of God made available by the work of Christ does not just lead to our being 'accounted' or 'reckoned' righteous before God. It also leads to an imparting of Christ's righteousness so that 'we become the righteousness of God' (2 Cor. 5:21).

Much ink (and blood) has been spilt on how exactly imputation and impartation relate. The Lutheran–Roman Catholic agreement on justification, however, gives us some hope that all Christians can together affirm that Christ is in his person our righteousness (1 Cor.1:30). The sinner is granted righteousness before God in Christ through the declaration of forgiveness but God's forgiving grace also brings with it the gift of new life through the presence of Christ within us. Indeed, the inclination to sin and even actual sin continue to be found in believers, even in those who are exemplary (Rom. 7) but if they confess their sin, God is faithful and just and will forgive them their sin (1 Jn. 1:9). Hans Küng has pointed out the ecclesial dimension of justification and sanctification and it is important to guard against an overly individualistic view of these fundamental doctrines. Righteousness is a characteristic of God's covenant people and the individual is accounted righteous and becomes righteous within the company of God's holy people (Ex. 19:6; 1 Pet. 2:9–10).[21]

John Henry Newman, who so struggled with the ways in which different traditions had understood the relation of the atonement to our justification, has left us, in successive stanzas, a summary of how Christ is to be understood as our representative, substitute, exemplar and victorious saviour:

O Loving Wisdom of our God!
When all was sin and shame,
A second Adam to the fight
And to the rescue came.

O wisest love! That flesh and blood,
Which did in Adam fail,
Should strive afresh against their foe,
Should strive and should prevail.

O generous love! That he who smote
In man for man the foe,
The double agony in man
For man should undergo;

And in the garden secretly,
And on the cross on high,
Should teach his brethren, and inspire
To suffer and to die.

We have seen how by faith and through baptism we are incorporated into the new humanity brought about by Christ's
sacrificial death and its wonderful vindication by God. This is
necessarily a once-for-all event, though the grace received then
continues to be operative throughout the Christian life and,
indeed, from time to time brings about its renewal.

The other great sacrament connected specifically with
Christ's atoning death is, of course, the Supper of the Lord,
Holy Communion or the Eucharist, whatever we wish to call it.
Recent biblical, historical and ecumenical scholarship has cast a
flood of light on how the cross relates to the sacrament and I
have myself considered the issue from a number of points of
view.[22] This is not the time to repeat what I have said elsewhere
except to say that according to the New Testament, the Lord's
Supper is not merely a memorial of a past event but has very
much to do with making the unrepeatable offering of Christ on
the cross effective for us today. In this sense, as the apostle Paul
reminds us, drawing an analogy with Jewish and Gentile
sacrificial meals, the Eucharist is a feasting upon Christ's
sacrifice (1 Cor. 10:14–22). The language about the blood of the
covenant (Mt. 26:28; Mk. 14:24) or of the *new* covenant (Lk.
22:20; 1 Cor. 11:23–26) evokes directly the sacrificial language of
Exodus 24:8, and Hebrews 13:10 is usually taken to mean
Christian participation in the Lord's Supper. As the Reformers
sometimes put it, partaking of Holy Communion is a receiving
of all the benefits of Calvary for ourselves. The sacrifice on
which we feast in a heavenly and spiritual manner is also the
ground of our pleading, which is joined to the continuing
intercession of Jesus our great High Priest (Rom. 8:34; Heb.
7:25). As John 6 teaches, and as Article 28 of the Articles of
Religion affirms, we truly partake of the body and blood of
Christ but *sacramentally*, thus excluding any crudely material
sense of such participation.[23] The ARCIC Final Report puts it
thus:

Becoming does not here imply material change. Nor does the liturgical use of the word imply that the bread and the wine become Christ's body and blood in such a way that in the Eucharistic celebration his presence is limited to the consecrated elements. It does not imply that Christ becomes present in the Eucharist in the same manner that he was in his earthly life. It does not imply that this becoming follows the physical laws of this world. What is here affirmed is a sacramental presence in which God uses the realities of this world to convey the realities of the new creation.

Quite so, and we can say amen to such a sacramental understanding of the Lord's Supper.[24]

The cross of Christ is unique. In the Book of Common Prayer it is referred to as 'a full, perfect and sufficient sacrifice, oblation and satisfaction, for the sins of the whole world'. No one else but the eternal Word of God himself could rescue us from our plight by assuming our nature, standing in our place and offering a sacrifice of obedience to turn away God's just anger from us and to make us friends, once again, with him. We have also seen that the implications of the cross are *universal*. It is 'for the sins of the whole world'. Nothing is untouched by it and all are brought to judgement under it but also to salvation through it if they respond with faith and love. The cross has significant implications for the transformation of individuals and of societies. These have also to be worked out in the economic, social and political spheres in terms of reconciliation, healing and justice. All of this depends, however, on taking an objective view of the atonement, which holds that a fundamental transaction between God and humanity has been completed. As a result, the impasse caused by sin has been broken and, at least potentially, humanity has been restored to that fellowship with God that was so rudely shattered by the primal sin. Christ has done it all for us and it is for us to respond in trust and thankfulness.

By his vindication of Jesus in bringing him back from the dead and raising him to glory, God has shown how Jesus has been made both Saviour and Lord. He is, of course, Lord of all but it is particularly his lordship of culture that we shall next address. This issue is, as we all know, crucial to the future of the Christian faith in a fast-changing world.

4

Lord of All: Christ, Culture and Context

'If Christ is Lord at all, he must be Lord of all,' as is often said. Through Christ's reconciling work on the cross, not only have we the possibility of being friends with God, sons and daughters brought back into the household, but the curse on the world brought about by our rebellion can also be lifted (Rom. 8:18–25). The new life bursting forth from the empty tomb is a foretaste of the transformation that God wills for the whole of the created order.

As the good news of what God was doing through the risen and glorified Jesus spread to different parts of the world, and as men, women and children were incorporated into this unstoppable movement, the question naturally arose as to the relationship of the gospel to the various cultures to which these people belonged. Were these cultures under God's judgement? Was there anything in them that had prepared people to recognize God's work when they saw it? Could these cultures be redeemed and was the Jesus movement a completely distinct culture from all of the rest?

As we shall see, some, at least, of these questions began to be addressed from early times. Let us begin, however, by asking what we mean by culture. Cultural anthropology and sociology have provided a wide range of definitions, descriptions and experiences of culture. It can be said, for example, that culture is about how people influence and, to some extent, alter their environment. It is also about how individuals and communities adapt and develop. Again, it could be said that culture is about the provision of social meaning. It has to do with the world view, the values and the idiom of particular groups. Traditions, customs, language all belong, in one way or another, to culture. As anthropologists have seen, it has to do with the non-biological heritage of humanity and, however it may be expressed, it is a leading characteristic of human beings wherever they may be found.[1]

The Second Vatican Council's Pastoral Constitution on the Church in the Modern World, *Gaudium et Spes*, speaks of culture as everything that contributes to the refining and developing of humanity's diverse mental and physical endowments. Through knowledge and work, women and men achieve mastery over nature, they develop social patterns of life in the family and in the wider community and they give expression to their spiritual experiences and aspirations.[2]

We can say at once that in the senses described above, culture is God-given and is grounded in the story of creation where man and woman are together created in God's image and given a common mission of stewardship in God's world, a mission that they are to fulfil in their respective ways (Gen. 1:26–30; 2:18–25). Human relationships, thought, spiritual awareness, material artefacts, all can be integrated when culture is seen as providential. Culture, then, is to be regarded as part of God's creative work, of which human creativity is a result.[3]

As we have seen, however, we are also conscious of a great disruption: human conflict, cruelty, the oppression of the weak, the exploitation of the poor, the distortion of marriage and the family, environmental degradation, corruption of different kinds and, most of all, the absence of meaning and significance in human life are truly, as Newman saw, a vision 'to dizzy and appal'.[4] The passages on creation, stewardship and blessing in the book of Genesis are followed immediately by an account of the Fall, of wilful disobedience and its consequences for the individual, for human relationships, for work and for the world as it is affected by human sin (Gen. 3:8–20). There can be no adequate account of culture that does not take such a comprehensive fallenness into consideration.

If we are to see culture as given by God for the sake of human flourishing, we have also to recognize that human beings have turned it into a vehicle for selfishness, greed and, above all, idolatry, that is, a systematic replacement of God and his gracious purposes with human constructs, ideas and ideologies. In such circumstances, we have to ask not only how culture can provide points of preparation and of connection with the gospel, but also how the gospel judges culture and, further, whether the gospel can redeem culture as well as individuals.

Charles Kraft emphasizes the interactional and incarnational aspects of the gospel's relationship to culture. Not only does God speak to specific groups of people in distinctive ways attuned to their language and cultural forms, but also in Christ he identifies completely with the human condition. Such models of what he calls 'receptor-oriented revelation' should also be paradigms for our own mission. He agrees that the arrival of the gospel in a particular culture brings about a transformation of the world view of that culture, but he wants to argue that it should be from the inside, gradual and 'with the grain' of the culture.[5]

It is certainly true that some of the so-called kerygmatic speeches in Acts attempt to relate the coming, the dying and the rising of Jesus to the history and the expectations of the Jewish people (Acts 2:14–36; 3:17–26; 7:2–53; 13:16–41, etc.). It is interesting to see, however, that Peter takes a somewhat different approach in his speech to the household of Cornelius (Acts 10:34–43), acknowledging that God shows no partiality but accepts those of every nation who fear him and do what is acceptable to him. St Paul, similarly, in addressing the people of Lystra, speaks in ways that would be more easily understood by them as he reminds them of God's general providence and also of his coming judgement.

The *cause célèbre* in this connection is, of course, Paul's speech on the Areopagus at Athens where he attempts to relate the gospel not only to what the Greek poets had said, but also to the cults that he saw around him (Acts 17:22–31). The poetic passages seem originally to have been addressed to Zeus, but Howard Marshall observes that at this time a process of 'demythologization' was already under way and that Zeus now stood for *Logos* or that universal Reason that was inherent in the structure of the universe and was also the source of moral guidance for humanity.[6] It is often said that Paul's speech at Athens was not immediately successful in winning a large number of converts but, as we shall see, its implications for a Christian approach to culture down the centuries can hardly be exaggerated.

This approach of attempting to connect with a people's cultural background continues in the period immediately following that of the apostles. In Justin Martyr's *Dialogue with Trypho the Jew* there is a sophisticated attempt to appeal to the Jewish Scriptures to establish the truth of Christ. Such a dialogical method draws on the Lucan account of the risen Lord's exposition of the Scriptures as he accompanies the two disciples on the road to Emmaus and when he makes himself known to the disciples gathered together (Lk. 24:13–27,32,44–47). Justin's approach is echoed in some other early Fathers, such as Tertullian and Origen.

The approach to the pagans is, however, constructed quite differently. It relies not so much on an appeal to the Scriptures as on notions that were generally current in the ancient world. What St Paul had done implicitly at Athens is made explicit by Justin's *Apology* to the Roman Emperor and the Senate. Christians are people of reason, according to him, because they believe in that universal Reason or *Logos* who is the creator of the universe, who inspired the prophets and who is incarnate in Jesus of Nazareth. Because Christians live in accordance with the teachings of Jesus, their lives are in stark contrast to the disorder, indeed, chaos, of the pagan world around them. Even before the coming of Jesus, this Reason was available to humanity to a greater or lesser extent. All those, whether Jews or Gentiles, who lived by its light can be acknowledged by Christians, while those who rejected it must be regarded as hostile.

Only a little later, Clement of Alexandria, in his *Protrepticus* or *Exhortation*, models himself on Paul's speech at Athens. For him, there is only one God, who has created the world by his all-powerful Word. This Word is both the cause of the 'music of the spheres', the harmony of the universe, and the one who implants in humanity a longing for God. This is the Word to whom the prophets bore witness. But Greek philosophy has also received some sparks of this Divine Reason, as has poetry, so that the power of truth cannot be hidden and in one way or another reveals itself to us.[7]

These early Fathers appeal to ideas of wisdom, justice and law that were current in the ancient world. Already in St Paul's letter to the Colossians the so-called 'household code' makes its appearance and is then seen in Ephesians, 1 Peter and elsewhere. Such codes were found widely in the ancient world and, indeed, in Judaism itself. In their use by Christians, they are distinguished by the stress on reciprocity: rather than all the duties being on one side and all the rights on the other, here we have rights and duties on all sides. Professor Charlie Moule has also pointed out that such reciprocity is grounded in the *en Christō* formula. Household life is so transformed 'in the Lord' that each person in it is seen as precious and each has obligations towards the others.[8]

It seems, then, that the Fathers recognized connecting points with the surrounding culture in the philosophy (especially of the Stoics), the poetry (of the Greek poets), the morality (of the household codes, for example) and even some aspects of prophecy among the Gentiles (for instance, of Sibyl, widely regarded as a divinely inspired source of truth and as witnessing to the coming of Christ).[9]

It would, however, be a very serious mistake to imagine that the Fathers had any kind of rosy view of the pagan culture to which they were speaking. Like the New Testament writers, they are entirely realistic about the limitations of approaches that sought connections and commonality between the gospel and the surrounding culture. Arne Rudvin goes so far as to say that the idea of the *Logos spermatikos*, the scattered Word, or, more accurately, the sowing Word, where it is used by the Apologists, for instance, Justin or Clement, is used to show how enlightened philosophers and thinkers were able to criticize and to refute popular religious notions and the culture of the day. According to him, it is never used directly to appeal to truth in a non-Christian religious tradition.[10]

It is certainly true that the very passages, for example in Clement of Alexandria, that show how the sparks of Divine

Reason among the poets led them to bear witness to the truth, also assert that pagan poetry is preoccupied by falsehood. In Justin, popular religiosity is attributed to demons, which work against the wisdom of people such as Socrates, who have been inspired by the *Logos* to turn the masses away from these demons. Popular morality is also said to be influenced by them and we are warned against the errors of philosophy.[11]

As in the Roman Empire, so also in the Persian, Christian apologists continued to give an account of their faith that both sought to connect with the culture in which they found themselves and also to critique it. Elsewhere I have mentioned the great Persian theologian and mystic, Bardaisan (known in the west as Bardesanes). In the west he is often regarded as a heretic and is associated with astrological fatalism. In his *Dialogue on Destiny*, however, written towards the end of the second century, we find him defending monotheism, human freedom and the distinctiveness of the Judaeo-Christian tradition, especially in its ethical dimension. Bishop William Young, the historian of the Church of the East, regards this apology as the earliest against the Magi known to history. Young sees his *Hymn of the Soul* as a kind of Eastern *Pilgrims Progress* and commends it as an expression of Persian Christianity.[12]

The providential aspect of human culture, its role in nurturing, guiding and governing human beings, individually and collectively, is recognized by diverse Christian apologists from the earliest period onwards. Its bondage, however, is also perceived, whether that be to human sinfulness or to supernatural powers. Culture is both affirmed and judged by the gospel. The Reformers of the sixteenth century, for instance, recognize that there is a spark of knowledge of God's will in human beings and that the divine law could be said to be inscribed on the human heart. They also hold, however, that such knowledge is distorted by fallen humanity and the law is obscured. A lack of knowledge of God's nature leads to a false understanding of his will. Human beings have some sense of what is demanded of them but not an accurate knowledge of the one who makes the demand. It can also be said that even if they recognize the moral demand on them, they are unable to meet what it asks of them. Without the good news of Jesus Christ, we are confronted with a moral and spiritual impasse.[13]

The debate on how much of culture has a connecting point with the will and purpose of God was re-ignited by Karl Barth and Emil Brunner in the middle of the twentieth century. The latter used the term *Anknüpfungspunkt* to claim that God reveals himself in nature and that even fallen humanity retains some 'point of contact' with God because human beings were made in God's image. He held that both aspects of the claim are necessary for there to be moral responsibility. Barth's 'no' to Brunner has been criticized by Oliver O'Donovan on the grounds that Barth fails adequately to distinguish between ontological and epistemological issues. In his quest for a proper epistemology, Barth denies certain aspects of the biblical teaching on creation that should never have been repudiated. Brunner, on the other hand, emphasizes the divine order and its claim on us not only in our natural, but also in our historical, existence. Within the latter, he includes the 'orders' of the family, the state, culture generally and even religion.

With Brunner, we can assert the existence and authority of the created order and acknowledge the imperfect knowledge of them that is retained by fallen humanity. With Barth, we can say that the existence and authority of the orders of creation can only be fully, definitively and really understood in the light of God's revelation in Jesus Christ and particularly in the newness that his resurrection from the dead brings to our understanding of these orders. This newness is not just a completion of what was known before but a radical remaking of it.[14]

The great American theologian H. Richard Niebuhr has attempted to provide a schema of the way Christ's relation to culture has been viewed by Christians down the ages.[15] In engaging with Niebuhr's categories, it is important to recognize that they are not wholly discrete but have some overlap. The Christ *of* culture represents those who believe that the gospel of Jesus Christ has ultimately provided the social underpinning for their society, and not only that, but that Christ is also the guide to cultural development and, indeed, is the goal towards which a particular culture, civilization or social order is moving.

We have seen already how the laws, institutions, values and customs of countries such as Britain and the United States can be seen as arising from a Christian vision and as sustained by the inculcation of virtues that are understood in a distinctively Christian way. Niebuhr points out that such an identification of Christ with western civilization is by no means the only example of the Christ of culture model. It can be seen in other ancient and modern situations. Among the former, Armenia, Ethiopia and the Maronites of Lebanon come to mind. Among the latter, the effects of Christianization on many African societies could be cited.[16] It is important, in this connection, to remember that in this model we not only see the Christian faith providing the basis for a civilization's values, institutions and laws, but also a means of critiquing a nation or civilization when it fails to live up to the biblical vision of justice, compassion and peace. It should not, therefore, on any account, be seen as simply endorsing what may happen to go on. Rather, it gives a Christian response informed by the gospel.

Second in Niebuhr's scheme, is the Christ *above* culture view of the relationship between gospel and culture. Here cultural institutions are seen as grounded in natural law and are recognized as being of divine providence but the spiritual longings and destiny of human beings also require supernatural revelation, which leads to salvation. The orders of creation and redemption are complementary and nature, even fallen nature, can prepare us for grace, which fulfils and completes nature, both having their origins in God's purpose for the world in Christ.

Martin Luther and, subsequently, Lutheran ethics typify the 'Christ and culture in paradox' view. Here there is a clear divide between the two kingdoms, the inner and the outer: in the external kingdom the divine law as revealed, for example, in the Decalogue, is enforced by duly constituted authority (Rom. 13:1–7). This is for the sake of vital social institutions such as the family, government, the workplace and organized religion. The other kingdom is that of faith, which brings justification and peace with God. On this view, it is the converted person who works in the social environment with a new disposition, with the fruit of the Spirit, as it were (Gal. 5:22–23). This leads to sacrificial service and to forgiveness but even these are not to be regarded in any way as contributing to a person's salvation, which is always by grace through faith.

The Christ *against* culture model is the one that seems most diametrically opposed to the first category of Christ in or of culture. Here the gospel is seen as judging all that is corrupt in culture. Christians are to 'come out' of such a situation (2 Cor. 6:14 – 7:1) and to keep themselves pure. The leading metaphor here is light rather than salt. Even where cultural insights are affirmed, the gospel is the lens through which everything is viewed and in relation to which receives its value. The Church is a distinct and distinctive spiritual society and only by remaining so can it be light in the surrounding darkness. Inevitably, redemption is viewed as deliverance out of an evil, sinful and rebellious world. Christians are exiles and sojourners in a foreign land where they continue to sing the Lord's song but are scarcely understood by those who belong to this world (Phil. 3:20; 1 Pet. 1:1; cf. Ps. 137).

Niebuhr's final category is that of Christ as the transformer of culture. Here, the norms of culture and its values are recognized as originating in divine purpose but are seen as disordered because of fallen reason and the fallen moral disposition. The vision of the good in Christ is to be used, then, to restore the corrupted order. The gospel brings about a new society, the Church, but this is for the sake of the rest of humanity since the purpose of God, in Jesus Christ, is the transformation of society and, indeed, of creation itself. This transformation has to do with the coming of the Eternal City and of a new heaven and a new earth (Rev. 21:1–5,22–27; 22:1–5; cf. Rom. 8:18–25).

It is to be emphasized that these categories are not necessarily mutually exclusive but may be complementary or successive, depending on the situation in which Christians find themselves. It is, for instance, quite possible to regard one's culture as based on a Christian world view and yet also to acknowledge another realm of spirituality that has to do with the sustaining of personal faith. In the same way, if a particular culture is seen to be moving away from its Christian moorings to a different world view, or even the absence of one, we also could legitimately make a move from predominantly Christ of culture categories to a Christ against culture way of evaluating developments in a society or civilization. In many situations in the majority world, the Church's involvement in development, or in bearing prophetic witness in the context of an oppressive political regime, leads naturally to the Christ as transformer of culture model. Here, what is true and God-given is affirmed but all that causes the corruption of an ordered human society is challenged and Christians are called to work for change and transformation according to the pattern of Christ.

David Gitari, the former Archbishop of Kenya, in a landmark address to the 1988 Lambeth Conference on evangelization and culture, distinguished between the different ways in which the gospel relates to culture. There are some aspects of culture, he said, that the gospel affirms and strengthens. The examples he gives, citing Bishop Stephen Neill, have to do with African awareness of human solidarity or *ubuntu* ('I am because we are'), hospitality and artistic creativity. There are other aspects, such as the custom among some tribes of men and women meeting separately, and, controversially, polygamy, which the gospel can tolerate for the time being in the hope that Christian teaching will bring about change. There are yet others to which the gospel is completely opposed, such as the practice in certain areas of twin-killing, cattle-rustling and, of course, witchcraft and sorcery. He goes on to explain how this view of gospel and culture is used in the Church's missionary work in Northern Kenya among the nomadic peoples there.[17]

Some of Gitari's views in this area can be and have been criticized. African Christians are increasingly realizing that *ubuntu* is double edged. It can certainly be useful in large-scale evangelism, where what is being sought is not just individual conversions, but the Christianization and discipling of a whole clan or tribe. On the other hand, a sense of solidarity can also prevent or retard that transformation of a person or community that the good news should bring about. Again, while there has been some sympathy with the view that polygamous men should not be made to put away all but one of their wives before being baptized, other proposals of Gitari have been received more critically. Allowing polygamous men to retain their wives on baptism, as long as they agree to take no more, is seen as good missionary practice and also as compassionate. Often when women were put away under missionary pressure, they became destitute and fell into evils such as prostitution. This must, however, be a strictly temporary provision for one generation alone. When Gitari claims that the Bible does not teach monogamy as God's will for human beings and for society, he is going too far. Monogamy is implicit in the creation narratives and in Jesus' use of them (Genesis 1:27f.; 2:23f.; Mk. 10:1–12 and parallels). It is difficult to imagine that important passages such as 1 Corinthians 7 or Ephesians 5:21–33 can have anything but monogamy in mind. Besides, being once married, with the possibility of a second marriage on the death of the spouse or, in some cases, after divorce, is a universal norm in the Early Church.[18]

While Gitari can be criticized for some of the examples he has chosen, he is surely right in the principles he enunciates regarding the relation of the gospel to culture. We need continually to seek those elements in any culture that can be affirmed and fulfilled by the gospel and while refusing to pass judgement too quickly, we must be alert to those aspects of culture that are challenged and opposed by the gospel.

Professor Lamin Sanneh, who is a convert to the Christian faith from a West African background, has drawn our attention repeatedly to what he calls the intrinsic translatability of the gospel.[19] From the very beginning, the message that is Jesus was translated first into Greek, and then into an exponentially growing number of languages around the world. It is interesting that the translation of the New Testament into Syriac (the language nearest to the Aramaic of Jesus) was not made until well into the second century. Such 'intrinsic translatability' can be compared with the irreducible 'Arabic-ness' of the Qur'ān, the *Adhān* (the call to prayer) and the *Salāt* (the Muslim ritual prayer). There are, of course, many translations of the Qur'ān but they are just that. They have no canonical authority. Like Christianity, Islam is a worldwide faith and in many respects it has come to be at home in the contexts of many languages and customs in different parts of the world. There is, however, a core of 'Arabness' about it that cannot be denied. According to Sanneh, this is not so for the Christian faith, which can be completely rendered not only into the languages, but also into the world views, idioms and thought-forms of the various cultures it encounters. In particular, Sanneh has studied the impact that various Bible translations have had when they have been translated into the languages of different African societies. Those who did the work of translation could hardly have been aware of the forces they were unleashing as they made the Bible available in those languages.

Sanneh's thesis has been significantly influential in recent missionary thinking but two caveats need to be entered. One is that the gospel cannot, of course, be rendered into the terms of any culture in such a way as to lose its capacity to judge that culture where it falls short of God's purposes for humanity. The other is that the gospel itself produces a culture and those who take it from place to place are formed by it. In other words, we can say that in the process of evangelization, the culture of the Church insofar as it is formed by the gospel, encounters another culture and that both are affected, influenced and, indeed, transformed by that encounter. This aspect of the Church's relation to culture was drawn to our attention when the then Cardinal Ratzinger addressed the presidents and other officials of the Asian Bishops Conference in 1993. According to him, faith is conveyed by the community of faith which, in turn, is formed by it. The encounter of the culture of faith with another culture does not seek to destroy that culture but to enable it to find its own centre. At the same time, such an encounter is an occasion for the renewal of the community of faith precisely because of the encounter.[20]

As Pope Benedict XVI, in his now famous Regensburg Lecture, he has once again raised the question of inculturation.[21] His remark about the relationship with Islam, which grabbed all the headlines, raises important issues about freedom of expression and how dialogue between Muslims and Christians should be conducted. It would have been quite possible to have raised these questions in other, less controversial, ways. From our point of view, however, it is the attention that the Pope gives to the Christian encounter with culture that is of importance. He rightly sees the encounter with Hellenism as providential, even if it is doubtful that Acts 16, with its story of the call to Macedonia, will bear the burden he places on it. Terms like 'Asia' and 'Europe' are not to be used anachronistically and nearly the whole area of St Paul's missionary activity, whether on the continent of Asia or of Europe, was highly Hellenized at the time. The very foundation myths of Europa and of Zeus show civilization arriving at this north-western end of the Eurasian land mass from south-west Asia. The fact of the matter is that the ancient world was spread over three continents (Africa, Asia and Europe) and there was considerable linguistic, cultural and philosophical movement across it (Aramaic and Greek, for example, were used as far away as Gandhara in what is now north-west Pakistan). The so-called mystery religions (many of oriental origin) were also important vehicles for spiritual, moral and social ideas.

In spite of these reservations, however, we can agree that the encounter with Hellenism was hugely significant for the development of the Christian Church and the Christian faith. It is to be noted, of course, that the Pope does not mean Hellenism in all its different manifestations but, rather, the 'purified' Hellenism of the philosophers. It is undoubtedly true that it was from such a Hellenism that the Church acquired the philosophical tools that enabled it to locate its message precisely in the situation at which it had arrived.

Two points need to be made here. The first is that the encounter with Hellenism took place at the popular, as well as at the philosophical, level. Part of the success of Christianity was that it was able to supplant not only many oriental cults, but also Hellenistic cults. An example of the latter are the cults of Neo-Platonist inspiration in Syria, which had posed a serious challenge to early Christianity. Such cults were often replaced not by accommodation and assimilation, but by vigorous opposition.

The other point is that Islam too had its encounter with Hellenism, largely through Christian mediation. Greek philosophical, scientific and theological texts were studied, commented upon and used very widely by Muslims. Both directly, and through the impact of Christian theology, Hellenistic ideas exerted a formative influence both positively and negatively on the emergence of *kalām* (formal theology) in

Islam, particularly on matters to do with God's being, his relation to the world, our knowledge of God, human destiny and the problem of freedom.[22] In this sense, Christianity's encounter with Hellenism was not unique.

We can, of course, agree with the Pope that the synthesis of Christianity with purified philosophical Hellenism was providential for the Graeco-Roman world of later antiquity. But, if so, what about early Christian encounters with other cultures and traditions? Bishop William Young has shown in his *Patriarch, Shah and Caliph* not only how the Church expanded in the Persian Empire (the other superpower of the time), but also Christian engagement with typically Persian ideas such as astrological fatalism, the struggle between Good and Evil and the ultimate triumph of the Good.[23]

In Egypt, we have the iconic figures of Athanasius and Antony. Athanasius was the archetypically Hellenized theologian who was completely at home in Greek ways of thought and speech. Antony, on the other hand, seems not to have known any Greek at all. And yet the two men were very good friends and had a deep respect for each other. In the context of the Pope's claim that Christianity, in spite of its origin and 'some significant developments in the East', took its historically decisive character in Europe, we have to consider the rise of monasticism in the deserts of Egypt, Syria, Mesopotamia and Persia. During his second exile, Athanasius took some Egyptian monks with him to Rome and thus planted the seed of monasticism in the soil of Europe. A significant development indeed![24]

The stories, songs and sermons of the Desert Fathers (and, in some cases, Desert Mothers) show us an entirely oriental form of Christian faith and practice often untouched by any kind of Hellenism. It was of this kind of spirituality that a famous European scholar once said that when he got to know it, he realized why the Romans had hated Christianity so intensely. It is also worth pointing out that while Sufism (or Islamic mysticism) undoubtedly has deep roots in the Qur'ān and the *Sunnah* (practice of the Prophet of Islam), it certainly developed, according to both ancient and modern Muslim testimony itself, in close interrelationship with Christian monastic ideals. Sufism is of huge importance in a world where Muslims struggle with questions about their spirituality and the role it should have in enabling them to come to terms with modernity. Its relationship to Christian asceticism is, therefore, at least worth noting.[25]

Almost from the beginning there seem to have been two 'tempers' or approaches to the Church's theological task. One, which can be termed 'Alexandrian', is heavily influenced by the Christian–Hellenistic synthesis that the Pope seems to have in mind. It is characterized by Church Fathers such as Clement of Alexandria, Origen and, in the West, to some extent, Ambrose and Augustine. Its theological method can be described as speculative, dogmatic and deductive. The other is the 'Antiochene' school, typified by Diodore, Theodore of Mopsuestia and St John Chrysostom. It emphasizes the biblical, historical and inductive approach and is less interested in the synthesis with philosophy. Both approaches are valuable in the overall theological task of the Church and one should not be, unnecessarily, preferred over the other.

Armenia, the first nation to regard itself as Christian, created, at a very early date, a Christian culture quite distinct from the Greek or Syrian or Egyptian cultures. At about the same time, Ethiopia also emerged as a distinctively Christian nation and, later, Empire. In the fifth century, 'the Nine Saints' from Syria translated the Bible and patristic texts into Ge'ez, and this translation brought into being an Ethiopian kind of Christianity, which is quite different from anything else in East or West.[26] Such instances of the inculturation of the Christian faith into non-Hellenistic environments can, of course, be multiplied but if each is regarded as providential, we have to ask what lessons they have for the worldwide mission of the Church today.

Since the Second Vatican Council, the universal need for inculturation has been recognized and Pope Paul VI, in his 1975 exhortation *Evangelii Nuntiandi* , emphasizes the importance of the gospel's encounter with cultures at the deepest level so that there is profound transformation. It was John Paul II, however, who first mentioned the mutuality of the process, in his encyclical *Slavorum Apostoli*, written in 1985 to celebrate the eleven-hundredth anniversary of the evangelization of the Slav people. Not only did Saints Cyril and Methodius incarnate the gospel into the culture of the Slavs, but they also brought the riches of Slav culture into the Church. The theme of mutuality is echoed in the encyclical *Redemptoris Missio* (1991), which deals with the missionary mandate of the Church. The Church not only transmits her own beliefs and values, and enables what is good in cultures to be renewed from within, but also brings these peoples and cultures into her own community.

The present Pope is also keen for a proper process of inculturation to continue and to be extended. Already, as Cardinal Ratzinger, he had seen that the 'providential encounters' of the past are a resource for, and need to be taken up into, the encounters of the present. In the Regensburg Lecture, also, he pleads for an authentic inculturation, and in the 1993 address to the Asian Bishops Conference, he looks for a 'providential' engagement with the great cultures of India, China and Japan. While the Christian Church has been continuously present in India from the early centuries, and Christianity had a presence in China before the modern period, the engagement with the philosophical reasoning of the cultures has only just begun and needs to develop a great deal before it produces fruits that can be compared with the results of these encounters with Hellenism.

In *Redemptoris Missio*, John Paul II reminded the Church of two 'guiding principles' in the process of inculturation: one is that of compatibility with the gospel itself and the other is the need for fellowship among Churches. That is to say, the whole counsel of God, in terms of God's love and how that has been manifested in the story of God's people and particularly in Jesus Christ, the objective nature of Christ's reconciling work and the new life released by the resurrection and the coming of the Holy Spirit, cannot be compromised in relationship to any culture. The integrity of the apostolic teaching in its passing on, receiving and passing on again, across cultures and down the ages, has to be maintained and renewed. It is true that from time to time a particular culture or context will highlight some aspect of this teaching that has been neglected or obscured. The Church can then with joy recover this aspect for herself. When, however, a question arises as to whether something really is an aspect of the apostolic teaching, this can only be settled by an appeal to Scripture as the norm of this teaching. On the basis of the ancient canonical principle that what affects everyone must be decided by everyone, any such question that affects the whole Church must be decided by the whole Church. Those, moreover, who have the ministry of teaching have a special responsibility to show how a particular development is or is not consonant with the apostolic teaching (and especially with Scripture as its norm).

The encyclical points out that inculturation is a slow journey and the expression of the good news in terms of a particular culture has to be in harmony with its expression in other cultures and at other times. This means that those engaged in this task can never forget the importance of fellowship among the Churches and not do anything to harm the organic nature of that fellowship.

The World Council of Churches' programme on Gospel and Culture has proposed criteria for, rather than limits to, the process of inculturation. These have to do with how the mind of Christ or the sense of the Scriptures can be rendered into the idiom of a particular people, how it can be made intelligible for them and how it can inspire and inform them as they seek to live a Christian life. There is an emphasis here on the whole counsel of God rather than proof-texting, but also on how certain trajectories in Scripture connect with a particular group of peoples at a particular time in their history. The Exodus trajectory, for instance, spoke powerfully to the slaves in North America and elsewhere and today it speaks to the oppressed on many continents.

We have seen already how William Tyndale's, and subsequent, translations of the Bible into English were intrinsic to the Reformation project but also how they were hugely influential in the development of the English language. Such work was a necessary part of the Reformation in England and the title deeds of Anglicanism show a strong commitment to the vernacular principle, that is, to the idea that people should be able to express the faith and to worship in their own language. Both the Preface to the 1662 Book of Common Prayer and the Articles of Religion (e.g. Article 34) show this commitment and can be a charter for inculturation in the Anglican communion as a whole.

Anglicanism spread across the world in a number of ways. It expanded along with the emigration of English-speaking peoples to parts of the world such as North America, Australasia, parts of Africa and the Caribbean. As long as it remained limited to such people, there was little desire to change the forms in which it was exported, even if there was sometimes a sense of responsibility to other people around – the 1662 Book of Common Prayer, for example, provides for adult baptism partly on the grounds that this may be useful for the 'Natives in our Plantations, and others converted to the Faith'. In the seventeenth century, however, Bishop Stephen Neill is able to record only one baptism of an Indian according to the Anglican rite.[27]

From this provision for the care of their own people, there arose a desire to bring the good news to others. In Anglicanism, such a desire was given effect in both the High Church, later to be called the Catholic tradition, and in the Low Church, or evangelical tradition. The former was represented by the Society for Promoting Christian Knowledge (SPCK) and the Society for the Propagation of the Gospel (SPG) and the latter by the Church Missionary Society (CMS).

Taking the CMS first, the historian Peter Williams has often pointed out the commitment in the middle years of the nineteenth century of its secretary, Henry Venn, to the emergence of indigenous churches that were not alienated from the culture in which they were set. According to the CMS, the Prayer Book itself and the Articles of Religion provided for every local or national church to adapt its worship, government and outward organization to the style, patterns and expectations of the culture around it. In essentials, such a church would be at one with the worldwide church and would share the same faith as that of the missionaries who had brought the gospel to their land, but in language, music, dress, buildings and ways of decision-making for local needs it could be very different.[28]

Venn was not alone in such thinking. He himself greatly admired the American missiologist Rufus Anderson, and the ideas of both are echoed and developed in the work of Roland Allen, a mission theologian from a High Church background, who wanted the missionaries to attend to the methods of

St Paul. Allen was keenly aware of the similarities of context in which both St Paul and some modern missions operated. Rather than making people dependent on him, Paul concentrated on the emergence of appropriate local leadership and so, said Allen, should the missionaries of his time.

Allen is particularly associated with the articulation of the 'three-self' principle, which is implied by both Venn and Anderson. This stated that each church was to be self-governing, self-supporting and self-propagating. In an era where there was constant danger of becoming permanently dependent on mission-ary largesse, this was indeed a sound principle to bring to the attention of both missionaries and indigenous church leaders.[29] Strangely enough, it was vigorously taken up by Chinese Communist authorities as one of the conditions required for the continued toleration of the Christian Churches. As Philip Jenkins has shown, this requirement, which may have been intended to choke off external support for the Chinese Church, resulted, in fact, in its toughening up for the rigours that were to follow. In turn, this has been the basis for the Church's unexpected and dramatic growth, which continues today.[30]

Whatever the impetus, Anglicanism has certainly spread to many parts of the world and even in areas, such as Latin America, Korea and Japan, that have never been under British influence. Similarly, it is found in parts of francophone Africa and in former Portuguese possessions on that continent. As it has expanded, there has sometimes been a stubbornness in retaining English forms of liturgy, architecture and forms of government. There has also been a desire, however, to express the Christian faith in terms of the idiom of the people to which it has come. In Africa, for instance, this is most noticeable in the spontaneity of worship, even within the constraints of liturgy, and in the rhythms and harmonization of music. It can also be seen in patterns of leadership and in the emergence of a movement such as the Mothers' Union, which, in its energy, enthusiasm and commitment, is quite unlike anything seen today in churches in the West.

In India, on the other hand, there is both a growing recog-nition of the spiritual milieu created by Hinduism and a desire to go back to the ancient roots of Christianity in that country.

The close relations that the Anglican Church, and subsequently the United Churches, have had with the ancient Syrian tradition as represented by the Mar Thoma Church have led to the development of liturgies heavily influenced by the Eastern tradition. Colin Buchanan calls these 'contrived' but does not take account of the living presence of the Eastern Churches in India, which are an example for all Christians in that country. Nor can we neglect the influence such liturgical experiment has had on liturgical revision in the West, especially through the Book of Common Worship of the Church of South India.[31]

Many of the features of liturgical inculturation in India, such as the removal of shoes at the Eucharist, the wearing of saffron, the *Namaste* for the Peace, the giving of the *mangalasutra* (a kind of necklace) at weddings instead of, or in addition to, a ring, remind us of earlier attempts, such as that of the Jesuits Roberto Nobili and Constant Beschi. As with Nobili, so also with his near contemporary in China, Matteo Ricci (1552–1610); many of the problems faced by these pioneers, such as that of ancestor reverence, in Ricci's case, or the extent to which social distinctions can form the basis for church, in Nobili's, remain with us today.

In many parts of Asia and Africa, the Church faces questions about ancestors. Is reverence of them equivalent to worship? Can all ancestors be remembered or only 'faithful' ones? What place, if any, should this practice have in the liturgical life of the Church? Where Nobili's wrestling with caste is concerned, the desire in parts of Africa for single-tribe dioceses, for instance, or the reluctance in the churches of India, even today, for the castes to mix, show us the enduring nature of the problem we face. The scar of racial segregation (doctrinaire or pragmatic) in the churches of the USA is yet another example of the same difficulty.[32]

Some veteran missionaries, such as Donald McGavran, and the school that has arisen from their inspiration, have developed the so-called Homogeneous Unit Principle (HUP). This tells us that people tend to become Christians along with others from their background. In one sense, this principle simply enunciates what evangelists and missionaries have always known. This is why there are student missions, neighbourhood evangelism, initiatives to reach people in sport, medicine or law. It is also the case that Christians of a particular kind gather together for nurture and fellowship. The question is whether a sound principle in missiology can be applied to ecclesiology. McGavran's missiology was hammered out in the context of caste-ridden India. One reason why some of his thinking was opposed by biblically- and catholic-minded church leaders and missiologists was that it evoked, once again, Nobili's caste-based approach, not simply to evangelization but to being church. Outside the Indian context, the dangers, obviously, are of churches based on race or on particular kinds of socio-religious groupings such as converts to Christian faith from some other religious tradition.[33]

We can understand why the HUP has been opposed in a world and a Church already bitterly divided along ethnic, social and other lines. I have myself opposed it and have been noticed by some of its advocates as having done so.[34] Closer attention to the ecclesiology of the New Testament may, however, lead us to a more charitable, if still restricted, view of the HUP. It is now increasingly recognized that the household churches were a primary and important way of being church. Such churches, naturally, centred around one family and the head of such a family might lead the church or at least be its patron and protector. Even though the family would have been extended, including servants and slaves as well as blood relatives, it would still have provided the church with a 'family likeness' or a certain amount of homogeneity (Acts 12:12; Rom. 16:5;1 Cor. 16:19; Col. 4:15; Philm. 2). It has been pointed out that in certain circumstances, women could be heads of households and that this might have given them a position of leadership in such churches or at least patronage of them.[35] Such leadership was not possible at the level of the city or town church because women could not hold public office in those days. Be that as it may, the point, for the time being, is that household churches were characterized by homogeneity and that today also we might countenance homogeneous expressions of church on analogy with such household churches.

As we have seen, however, it seems that from the earliest days there were gatherings not only of those who were 'like' one another, but also wider gatherings (even if some still took place in a home) of those who were characterized by being 'unlike' one another or heterogeneous. The churches named at the head of various letters in the New Testament would then be examples of such gatherings in Rome, Ephesus, Corinth, Antioch, etc. In his instructions regarding the Lord's Supper, for example, St Paul recognizes that rich and poor will be present (1 Cor. 11:17–22). In the letter of James also there are clear instructions about treating people alike when they are from different social backgrounds (2:1–5). The controversy between Peter and Paul in Antioch, similarly, was about the need for fellowship between Jewish and Gentile Christians, who were unlike one another in terms of their religious background (Gal. 2:11–14). We know from the letters of Ignatius, from Justin and from much else besides how these mixed gatherings in a city or town became normative for an understanding of the local church.[36] If, therefore, there are those who seek fellowship with Christians from their own ethnic, religious, professional or social background, it is incumbent upon them also to seek the wider fellowship of those who are unlike them, and this on a regular basis. Only then will the need for both homogeneity and heterogeneity be satisfied.

St Paul's constant exhortations to Gentile Christians to help the churches in Judea (1 Cor. 16:1–4; 2 Cor. 8 – 9), the help sent by the church in Antioch to the famine-affected brothers and sisters in Judea (Acts 11:27–30), the greetings from one set of churches to others (e.g. 1 Cor. 16:19) and the instruction that a letter sent to one of the churches should be read by another (Col. 4:6), all show that fellowship was not restricted to the local church but, in fact, took place across cultural, racial and national boundaries. If the universal Church, for example in Ephesians and Colossians, is theologically prior to the local churches, we can say also that the local churches, in and from their relationship with one another, make up the universal Church.[37]

It was really the eighteenth-century Evangelical Revival that woke up the Church of England to its responsibility for world mission. It was not always so. Indeed, if a generalization were to be allowed, we could say that the Churches of the Reformation did not produce a sense of world mission. For all its faults, and in spite of many mistakes, the Counter-Reformation in the Roman Catholic Church did produce an impetus for mission and the history of the modern missionary movement can, more or less, be dated from it.[38]

Many reasons have been given for the failure of the Reformation Churches to engage in, or even think about, the worldwide mission of the Church. There was the lack of opportunity, at least in the early years, because the sea routes were controlled either by Roman Catholic powers or still by the Arabs. There was the theological dispensationalism of the theologians, which held that all the nations had been given the chance to hear and respond to the gospel and if God wished the heathen to have another opportunity, then *he* would provide the means. Most of all, however, it had to do with the ways in which these Churches came to be identified with a particular people (in this sense, they were folk churches), their ethnicity, the nation state and, subsequently, with the culture that emerged from the upheaval. The down or dark side of the engagement with culture was a kind of captivity to the culture of a particular group of people, resulting in a failure both to be adequately concerned for other groups and to be prophetic to the culture in which the Church was set. The circumstances of Reformation settlements made it intrinsically likely that churches would not be able to resist cultural change rigorously enough if it ran contrary to the gospel.

As far as Anglicanism is concerned, Ephraim Radner and Philip Turner have pointed out that the danger of capitulation to culture has always been there and it is only that present circumstances have revealed the full extent of the fault lines.[39] When Anglicanism began to spread across the world, this tendency was exported and is most pronounced where Anglicans have had a role in folk religion, civic life or political arrangements. If such a tendency is to be countered, and even turned around, we will have to be clearer about how the integrity of living, passing on and receiving the apostolic faith is maintained. What is the role of Scripture as the normative expression of this faith in such contexts? And how can an effective teaching authority be developed, one that encourages essays in exploration, interpretation and development but can, nevertheless, from time to time declare authoritatively what Christian teaching is in particular matters of belief or of living the Christian life? It is, of course, important to remember that apostolic integrity, and the structures for maintaining it and relating it to contemporary issues, cannot simply be invented wherever needed but belong, rather, to the nature of the Church of Christ and should develop in accordance with its freedom and order. It is for the Anglican and other Churches to make sure that the extent to which they are Churches of Christ is freely expressible and that, along with other Christians, they receive again elements of being church that they may have lost or that have become obscured, or been neglected or compromised.

Samuel Zwemer, the great missionary to the Muslim world, said, 'We must become Moslems (*sic*) to the Moslem if we would gain them for Christ.'[40] In saying this, Zwemer was, of course, echoing the missionary strategy of St Paul (1 Cor. 9:19–23). There are some missionaries and missiologists, however, who have followed McGavran, particularly in pressing to the limits the contextualization of the Christian faith and being church within the framework of another *religion*. Some have gone farther than others. While some have simply advocated evangelism that takes a particular religious tradition seriously and encourages Christians from a particular religious background not to break with the cultural concomitants of that background, others have pressed for a following of Christ *within* a particular non-Christian tradition of faith.[41]

All of this raises questions about the relation of the Christian faith to other religions. To what extent is a properly Christian view one of negation or of challenge, and to what extent one of connections and fulfilment? It is these questions that we shall address in the next chapter.

5

'Not far from any one of us': Christ and the Religions

I have remarked elsewhere that spiritual awareness seems to be innate in human beings. Research among children, with those outside the boundaries of organized religion and by those interested in a psychological or even physiological basis for religious experience, is increasingly showing us that the spiritual is not merely a cultural construct. Nor is it a virus that attacks and infects us from outside. It is, in fact, natural to the human condition and down the ages we have used it to make sense of our social and personal lives.[1]

As might be expected, sociologists have tended to emphasize the social function of religion and this has sometimes led them to be more interested in the formal, ritualistic and symbolic role of religions rather than the inward, personal and mystical dimension. Whatever the importance of the social, we cannot ignore the personal aspect of the spiritual. It is this that enables people to have meaning for their own lives and to understand, to a greater or lesser extent, the significance of the universe. It can bring out what is best in them but also what is worst. The greatest acts of altruism, of sacrifice and of generosity often have their wellsprings in this personal awareness of the spiritual but when it is distorted, it can also give rise to hatred, cruelty and conflict.

It is the social function of the spiritual, however, that can properly be described as 'religion', as a binding together (*religare*), and it is true that in all ages and for most cultures, religion has been the glue that has held a society together. It is sometimes argued that this cohesive role of religion is being overtaken by democracy and the welfare state since the latter provides all the services a society needs, and democracy furnishes the legitimating that is required without reference to any supreme being. It is, however, increasingly evident that democracy of itself can hardly provide all the legitimating that is needed, while the welfare state is discovering more and more the importance of the 'third sector', of which the faith communities are a significant part.

Religious ideas often lie at the root of social institutions and although moral awareness is by no means limited to 'religious' people, it is the great religions that have provided the moral codes, such as the Torah, the Sermon on the Mount, the Shariah and the Laws of Manu, which have undergirded and, in many cases, continue to influence, law-making and its implementation. More generally, the customs and values that are needed for the proper functioning of any society often have a spiritual basis that has been conveyed by a religious tradition. Denial that this is so either results in a great impoverishment of culture, with people living on 'past capital' but refusing to recognize its provenance, or in the elevation of derivative ideas that are themselves dependent on the primary tradition but are not recognized as such.[2]

Cohesion is, of course, very far from being the only social function of a religious tradition. At least some traditions also have the capacity to critique a particular society, its values (or lack of them) and the direction it is taking. The so-called 'religions of the book', Judaism, Christianity and Islam, have a strong prophetic element that is orientated to precisely this task. It is from such an element that the individual derives strength to challenge the community, the powerless the powerful, and the oppressed their oppressors. Other traditions can also do this. Both Buddhism and Sikhism were founded explicitly on the basis of a critique of the caste system, and within Hinduism itself there have been throughout history movements that have challenged caste.[3]

Both the personal and the social aspects of religion can go wrong, of course. In this, the spiritual aspect of our personal and corporate lives is no different from any other. Human relationships sour and can become damaging rather than nurturing. Patriotism, or love of one's country, is a wonderful and highly desirable attribute in citizens, but it can become inward-looking, chauvinistic and even racist. Entrepreneurial flair, similarly, is the very lifeblood of commerce, but it can easily become greedy and self-serving. Religion too can become a reason for hate and rejection, for exclusion and for a lack of communication. It can become an ingredient in powerful and destructive cocktails of chauvinistic nationalism and political ideology. In this, religion can be compared with other forces at work in society.

The major conflicts of the recent past have sometimes had religion as an element in them. We can think of the conflict in the Balkans or the partitioning of the great continent of South Asia or the 'troubles' in Ireland. The most serious, however, have been provoked by secular ideologies such as National Socialism, Stalinism, Mao Ze Dong's Cultural Revolution, Pol Pot and even Saddam Hussein's Ba'ath party. If religion is to accept some of the blame for violence and conflict, then so must others.

Having said that, it remains the case that the different faiths have a responsibility today for upholding world order and for the promotion of fundamental freedoms and enlightened citizenship. They are accountable at the bar of world opinion and they are accountable to one another. It will no longer do for religious traditions to plead autonomy and to adopt a 'self-contained' attitude. As I have pointed out, Islam and Christianity are the two great missionary faiths in the world today. They are expanding rapidly in many parts of this world. Such expansion has brought them cheek by jowl in many new areas and they have a grave responsibility for maintaining peace, harmony and cooperation in the societies where they find themselves in close juxtaposition. They also have a particular responsibility for world peace. In this, their representatives need to assist, inform and inspire those political leaders whose task it is to maintain and, if necessary, to restore peace in a particular part of the world. They need to be involved where issues of faith are at stake and, at the international level, they should be contributing significantly to matters such as the justifiability of conflict in certain circumstances, appropriate patterns of governance in different parts of the world, the relationship of religion to law, both nationally and internationally, and the promotion of educational, cultural and scientific exchange between countries and civilizations. Nor should we neglect the contribution they should be, and, indeed, are making to a new, more just economic order, as well as to issues of development.

If faiths are to make these contributions, which are being asked of them, they must have the spiritual, intellectual and moral capacity to do so. This brings us to the claims the different faiths make for themselves, how they understand the human condition and their views of the world, its destiny and purpose. Christians, naturally, will evaluate such matters from the perspective, and with the resources, of their own faith. Hopefully, they will not exclude themselves from such a critical evaluation but they will not hesitate to evaluate other faith traditions also. Only in this way can dialogue be genuinely informed and committed. It is, of course, impossible in the space of a single chapter to discuss all of the issues involved, even in relation to a single tradition. What we can do is lay out the criteria for such evaluations: What does the Bible say? How did the patristic Church deal with plurality? How does Salvation-History relate to God's universal purposes? What is the relationship between the truth of the gospel and any apprehensions of truth in the different religious traditions? What is the relationship between judgement and fulfilment and how does preaching recognize adequately the role of Providence? How does a proper doctrine of God assist us in our conversations with others?

It is perhaps appropriate to begin by saying that the Bible always condemns false religion. It categorically refuses, for example, to participate in Canaanite society, based as it was on the priest–king axis, and the exploitation by the powerful of the ordinary people in the land. It has been said that early Israel's monotheism was a function of the egalitarian nature of its society, but it can equally be claimed that it was the monotheism of Israel that led it to critique and then to reject unequal and oppressive social structures such as those of the Canaanites. As

John Goldingay declares, a properly radical theology and radical sociology go together.[4]

The Torah, the historical books, such as Joshua and the writing prophets repeatedly warn Israel against compromise with Canaanite religion and particularly its promiscuous and permissive aspects, which are seen as inherently degrading especially because of the cult prostitution practised within them. In this religion, women were seen mainly in sexual and fertility terms, thus obscuring their dignity as persons. Homosexual cult prostitution, similarly, was seen as contrary to the created order and as a violation of the God-given dignity of human beings.[5]

The pagan hierarchical system and the fertility cults are seen by the biblical writers as being at the service of idolatry, that is, worship of the creation rather than the Creator, whether in the form of an animal representing a god, as in the Egyptian and Baal cults, or of vegetation in the Asherah poles, which the Israelites were commanded to cut down and burn (Ex. 34:13; Deut. 12:3). But, of course, this idolatry is seen and rejected most clearly in the worship of images of the gods. Yahweh the God of Israel and the creator of the world cannot be portrayed in terms of his own creatures. The foolishness of even attempting this is mocked by prophets such as Deutero-Isaiah (40:18–20). Behind the critique of idolatry lies the profound concern of the biblical writers that the creation, whether in terms of its beauty, power or fruitfulness, should not be mistaken for the one who has brought it into being, sustains it at every moment and is fulfilling his purposes of judgement and salvation for it.

The Bible's condemnation of false or bad religion is not, however, the end of the story. Its response to people's spiritual awareness, however distorted and obscured by human sinfulness, is much more subtle than that. Two illustrations should suffice to show how nuanced this approach can be. There is, first, the story of Melchizedek (whose name means King of Righteousness), who appears to be a Canaanite priest-king, representing the very tradition that elsewhere the Hebrews are concerned to challenge and to reject (Gen. 14:17–24). He brings Abraham, the father of the faithful, a sacred meal and a benediction from *'El 'Elyôn* (God Most High). In his turn,

Abraham makes Melchizedek an offering. Here, the cult of 'El Elyôn is identified with that of Yahweh himself, especially as Abraham later on swears by Yahweh, 'El Elyôn (Gen. 14:22). According to Gerhard Von Rad, such an evaluation of a Canaanite cult is unparalleled in the Old Testament.[6] There is further reflection on Melchizedek in Psalm 110, one of the oldest in the Psalter, where the Davidic King and the coming Messiah are identified with the Canaanite priest-king. In the New Testament, Jesus himself refers to this psalm, indicating that the Messiah is more than just the Son of David (Mk. 12:35–37 and parallels). In the letter to the Hebrews, the high priesthood of Jesus is understood to be the royal priesthood of Melchizedek since it could not be that of Aaron (5:6; 7:17,21).

The other obvious example of 'Canaanization' is the building of the Temple. It is here that the change in Israel from a nomadic to a settled people is most clearly seen. The plan of the Temple, its architectural features, cultic provisions and artistic portrayals all owe a great deal to the Middle-Eastern context of ancient Israel and particularly its Canaanite surroundings.[7] The tension between the liberation of the Exodus and the settlement in Canaan, with its institutionalization and attendant compromises, remains in the rest of the Bible. The prophets continue to confront the institutions, both from the inside and the outside, and to advocate the wholeness of God's rule in cult, economy and social order. The 'politics of God' is thus constantly brought to bear on the politics of the nation.[8]

Melchizedek is, of course, a type of the Messiah but there are numerous other individuals and even peoples outside historic Israel who are shown in the Bible as having authentic spiritual awareness and response: there is, for instance, the curious incident of Balaam, a Mesopotamian prophet who is made by God to prophesy for Israel in the face of their enemies (Num. 22–24). Other parts of the Bible, in both the Old and the New Testaments, come to a very negative assessment of this person but it cannot be denied that he was inspired by God's Spirit and prophesied in a most remarkable way. Then there is Ruth the Moabitess who, because of her loyalty and obedience, becomes the ancestress not only of David, but of Jesus as well. Jesus himself reminds his hearers of Elijah being sent to the widow of Zarephath (1 Kgs. 17:8–24; cf. Lk. 4:25–26) and of Elisha healing Naaman the Syrian (2 Kgs. 5:1–19; Lk. 4:27). The latter story has a strange twist to it at the very end. After Naaman has been healed, he vows to worship only the God of Israel but then asks for pardon when he goes into the temple of Rimmon with his master, the king of Syria. Significantly, Elisha says to him, 'Go in peace.'

The book of Job is explicitly set outside the land of Israel and its main character is described as 'the greatest man among all the people of the East' (Job 1:3). Its use of archaic Semitic words and borrowing from other Semitic languages, such as Arabic, is unique. The casting of this work in a non-Israelite setting facilitates a humanistic and universal, rather than a historical or particular, perspective. Job, along with Noah and Daniel, the legendary Canaanite king, are three figures who are not Israelite but are, nevertheless, symbols of righteousness and mediators of truth for others in times of crisis (Ezek. 14:14,20).[9]

The book of Jonah, by contrast, is about an Israelite prophet who is sent to preach repentance to the Gentiles of the city of Nineveh. The story is full of surprises: Jonah refuses to go, the ship on which he is fleeing God's call is threatened with shipwreck, and when thrown overboard by the sailors, he is swallowed by a great fish, to be vomited out three days later. When Jonah does finally make it to Nineveh, his preaching is amazingly effective and the people of Nineveh repent, with the result that God does not punish them. But instead of being pleased, Jonah is cross that the oracle he has brought will not be fulfilled and his reputation will be in tatters. God has to show him that he is not only a God who judges, but also one who saves and that his saving purposes extend to the Gentiles.[10]

Melchizedek is not, of course, the only Gentile king who honours and praises 'God Most High'. The Aramaic section of the book of Daniel recounts the story of King Nebuchadnezzar of Babylon's humiliation and his subsequent restoration. When reason returns to the king his first act is to praise *'Illāya* (the Most High), who he later on also calls *Melek shemeya* (King of heaven) (Dan. 4:34–37). The interesting point both here and in the Melchizedek passage is that specific Israelite terms for God are not used, thus implying that these Gentiles were blessing

Israel's God, the creator of the world and the only God, in their own terms.[11]

In the second part of the book of Isaiah, Cyrus of Persia is called both God's shepherd and his anointed (Messiah) (Isaiah 44:28 – 45:7). God chooses him to be the divine agent, grants him success in his expeditions and uses him to liberate his people from their exile and captivity so that Jerusalem can be restored and the Temple rebuilt. Although Cyrus does not know Yahweh, the God of Israel, he will come to know something of his power through the liberation of Israel. Cyrus and the whole world will have to see Yahweh not only as the Lord of creation, but also as the Lord of history.[12]

The New Testament virtually opens with the journey and homage of the Magi to the child Jesus. The Magi were a traditional class of priest-astrologers from what is now Iran. They had been gradually absorbed into Zoroastrianism and, in turn, greatly influenced it. For St Matthew, the visit of the Magi represents the Messiah's significance for the Gentiles. In this connection, Timothy, Nestorian Patriarch of Baghdad in the eighth and ninth centuries, has this to say:

> We showed our faith openly in the persons of our envoys, who were guided by a star, and in the gifts which they offered to Christ – gold, as to the King of all kings and the Lord of all lords; frankincense, as to the one who is God over all; and myrrh, to signify the passion of his humanity for our sake . . . Thirty years before all others we Easterns confessed Christ's kingdom and adored his divinity.[13]

The dimension of universality is also present in Matthew's description of the earliest phase of Jesus' ministry, which clearly included the Gentiles (4:23–25). Matthew and Luke both record the case of the centurion's servant who is healed by his master's faith in Jesus. Luke is at pains to tell us that this officer was already a God-fearer and had built the synagogue at Capernaum for the Jews. In Matthew, Jesus not only commends his faith as exceeding that of his contemporary Israelites, but also makes it a basis for speaking of the universal scope of the coming kingdom of God (Mt. 8:5–13; Lk. 7:1–10; cf. Jn.4:46–54).

Both Mark and Matthew report Jesus' encounter with the Syro-Phoenician woman (interestingly called a Canaanite by Matthew, perhaps alluding to the ancient enmity between the Canaanites and Israel, Mt. 15:21–28; Mk. 7:24–30). Here, Jesus clearly affirms the unique vocation of Israel as an instrument of God's universal purposes. It is through the renewal of Israel that God's purposes for his world are to be fulfilled. The woman's humble and touching faith is, nevertheless, in stark contrast to the growing hostility of the Jewish leadership, both religious and political. This may well have been a turning point in Jesus' ministry in terms of how he saw the Gentiles responding to the gospel. As with the Magi, the centurion, the Samaritan leper and the woman of Samaria, here was faith in him that was not easily seen in 'Israel after the flesh'. The evangelists certainly report this difficult story, as they do the others, as an example of the possibility of Gentiles, even from degraded and idolatrous backgrounds, being able to respond to God's revelation in Christ. Each of these encounters of Gentiles with Jesus is an indication of the great universal mission that is to come in the wake of the cross, resurrection and ascension of Jesus and the subsequent outpouring of the Spirit on the disciples.

As we have seen, the story of Cornelius in the Acts of the Apostles is an extremely important watershed in the account of the earliest mission of the Church. The story is first told in the whole of chapter 10. It is then retold in chapter 11 as Peter defends himself when he is charged with socializing with Gentiles. There is also a summary of it in Peter's speech at the Council of Jerusalem (15:7–9). All of this suggests that the event deals with a decisive issue. Cornelius is described as a 'God-fearer' who worships the God of Israel but is not formally part of Israel as he has not become a proselyte. His prayers have been heard by God and Peter opens his speech by acknowledging this: 'I now realize how true it is that God does not show favouritism but accepts men from every nation who fear him and do what is right' (10: 34–35).

Even more significantly, Cornelius is not alone. He has gathered together his family and close friends. Peter preaches the gospel to all of them and the Spirit falls on 'all who heard the message' (v. 44). This is clearly a direction-changing moment for the Early

Church. They are now able to say with Peter, 'God has granted even the Gentiles repentance unto life' (Acts 11:18). Questions about whether such Gentiles should be circumcised, what ritual and food laws they should be required to observe if Jewish-Christians were to have fellowship with them, etc. all arose from this single, stunning event in the ministry of St Peter. Not only the Council of Jerusalem, but also the rest of the New Testament writings can be said to be grappling with the issues raised here and by the continuing response of Gentiles to the gospel.

Again, in Acts 14, the people of Lystra want to give divine honours to Paul and Barnabas because they have healed a cripple. They prevent this by crying out that they are mere mortals and are bearing witness to the one true God who has not left himself without witness anywhere. As we have noticed already, Luke highlights the particular aspects of this speech that are orientated towards a Gentile audience: in the past God allowed people to go their own way, nevertheless, they had evidence of his existence because of the good things he had provided for them (cf. Rom. 1:19–20). Now, through the good news being preached by the apostles, God is calling everyone to a living relationship with him.

The speech to the people of Lystra is closely related to Paul's much better known address to the Athenians (Acts 17:22–31). In assessing this speech, it is crucial to try to steer between those who emphasize its negative aspects in relation to religious beliefs and those who claim that it sanctions a positive evaluation of such beliefs. It is important to note that Paul's spirit was 'provoked' within him as he saw the idols at Athens. The term *paroxunō* could mean either that he was angry and grieved at the idolatry or that he was moved to try and convert the Athenians. It was this movement in his spirit that led him to reason, discuss and argue (*dialegomai*) both in the synagogue with the Jews and 'God-fearers', and in the *agora*, or market place, with the general populace of Athens. It was this activity that led to his being seized by the Epicurean and Stoic philosophers and frog-marched to the court of the Areopagus so that he could be more closely examined on his precise teaching.

Some have held that in trying to use intellectual arguments to win over intellectuals, Paul made a bad mistake and his speech on the Areopagus was a failure. That is why, when he arrived next in Corinth, he decided to preach nothing but 'Jesus Christ and him crucified' (1 Cor. 2:2). Others have said that what Paul was trying to do was to set out his beliefs in a thought-provoking way, which yet sought to establish as many points of contact as possible with the beliefs of his audience. Nor can this approach be called a failure. He won some notable converts and his teaching was to bear much fruit later on as the Church began to grapple with the intellectual challenge from the Gentile world.[14]

The dedication of altars to unknown gods seems to have been a kind of insurance policy in case devotion to a god had been inadvertently left out. Paul seizes on this to proclaim, once again, that the God who is unknown, but should have been known through his goodness in creation, is the one who has been made known in the Jesus of the gospel he is preaching. A very clever balance is struck in appealing to something even in the polytheistic culture of Athens while, at the same time, challenging the cults of idols in a way that would have made sense to both the Epicureans and the Stoics.

Bishop Lightfoot, in one of his appendices to his definitive commentary on the letter to the Philippians, points out the affinities with, and dependence on, oriental thought that Stoicism has manifested and claims that it is that which provides the ground for similarities with Christianity and this to such an extent that Stoicism can be regarded as the precursor of the Christian faith in the Graeco-Roman world.[15] Paul's well-known use of pagan Greek poetry is also to be understood in this context. As we have noted already, the original reference to Zeus in the words used (they are not exact quotations): 'For in him we live and move and have our being' and 'We are his offspring' (Acts 17:28) had already been modified by the Stoics to mean the *Logos*, or the universal Reason, which provided the deep structuring of the universe and the basis of human morality.[16]

Paul is prepared to use characteristically Stoic ideas to promote the cause of the gospel. In this, he is the first but certainly not the last. We have seen already, in Chapter 4, how the second-century Apologists began to relate to the pagan world around them. In the Diaspora they had available to them as, indeed, it had been to Paul, the tradition of Jewish apologetics. They were glad to affirm aspects of Stoic philosophy as providing an explanation for an ordered universe that was consonant with biblical teaching. Again, the ethical concern of the Stoics resulted in a practical morality that found resonances in the moral world view of the Bible. As we have seen, even pagan poetry, in spite of its being regarded as degraded by Christians, could be used and, strange as it may seem, so could the desire among the Stoics for the prophetic. Clement of Alexandria, for example, is able to begin his excursus on prophecy with a reference to the Sibylline oracles, which he certainly regarded as of pagan origin but which were thought to prophesy of Christ.[17]

Such a positive evaluation of the religio-cultural *Weltanschauung* should not detract from the severe criticism of false religion that is to be found in the Bible – in the New Testament as much as in the Old. Jesus himself repeatedly draws our attention to the difference between authentic and spurious forms of spirituality and devotion (e.g. Mt. 6:1–18; 23; Jn. 4:19–24). Kenneth Cracknell is entirely correct when he states that the human world of religion is always ambiguous and open to demonic influence. There can be no rapport between the evangelist and false religion such as that of Simon Magus (Acts 8:9–24), the owners of the slave girl with a spirit of divination at Philippi (Acts 16:6–19), the seven sons of Sceva (Acts 19:11–17) or the silversmiths at Ephesus (Acts 19:23–41).[18] And as we have seen in Chapter 4, Bishop Arne Rudvin has shown that in Justin Martyr and other early Apologists, the idea of the *Logos spermatikos* (the scattered or sowing Word), is used not so much to evaluate religious traditions positively as to account for criticisms of them both from within the traditions themselves and from without.[19]

It is now widely recognized that much of the pattern of biblical thought has to do with the conviction that God is working out his purposes of judgement and salvation for humanity, and for the created order as a whole, through the calling, obedience, rebellion, punishment and restoration of Israel. It is this Salvation-History, in which God is seen to be active among his people and in his world, that is brought to a climax in the coming, teaching, working, dying and rising again of Jesus of Nazareth and that continues on in the story of the Church, those who were not a people but now, by grace through faith, are God's people (1 Pet. 2:10). It is rightly held that this Salvation-History is normative for our understanding of the human situation and God's remedy for it.

The question, however, is this: If biblical Salvation-History is normative, does it enable us to discern where and how else God is acting savingly? In fact, the Bible itself gives us some clues as to how this may be happening. As I have noted elsewhere, it is in the so-called 'writing prophets' that the Salvation-History, as seen in the story of Israel, is beginning to be linked with the stories of other peoples, which can in some respects be seen as their 'salvation-histories'.[20] That is to say, they can tell us something about how God is preparing them for revelation of himself. Thus, in Amos, ways in which God has worked in the past among people both far away and near to Israel, are explicitly related to the defining event in the story of Israel: the Exodus. These other people too have a history of salvation, even if they are unaware of it. Their stories too have to be seen in the context of God's plan. Those farthest away and most different, the Ethiopians, are as much part of this plan as those who may be the nearest (such as the Arameans). Israel's friends and foes are all included. From the beginning, God has been working out his purposes among them (Amos 9:7).

The opening of the book of Malachi compares the reluctant, miserly and defective offerings of Israel with the worthier ones that even the Gentiles are bringing (Mal. 1:6–11). From the earliest times, attempts have been made to understand this passage as referring to the future (it was, for example, sometimes regarded as a prophecy of the Eucharist). Some translations of verse 11 put the verb into the future tense ('incense *will be* offered to my name, and pure offering'). Taking everything into account, however, it seems that the prophet is referring to contemporary events even if a reference to an imminent future cannot be excluded. The sense would then be that even the distorted view of God and of his worship to be found among the Gentiles is better than, or is very soon going to be better than, the corrupt offerings of his chosen people. A severe indictment, indeed. But is there some recognition here of an acknowledgement of the true God even in the midst of Gentile superstition – an acknowledgement that can be purified and fulfilled?[21]

Tendencies in the earlier part of the book of Isaiah stem, of course, from the plural contexts in which the people of Israel found themselves from time to time. In Isaiah 19 there is a moving vision of universal peace with open borders and with former enemies living amicably together. It is, however, the closing verses that are the most remarkable, for here Israel and her former foes are together a blessing for the earth. That this is an eschatological vision is shown by the repeated formula 'in that day'. A time is coming when Yahweh himself will say, 'Blessed be Egypt my people, Assyria my handiwork, and Israel my inheritance' (19:25).[22]

A people's salvation-history has to do with what God has done in the past, what he is doing now and his plan for their future. None of this can be understood without reference to Salvation-History as it is recorded in the Bible. It is this inspired, and inspiring, record of God's dealings with humanity and with his creation that allows and enables us to discern how God is preparing a particular people, with a specific history, customs and spirituality, for the fulfilment of his purposes, which he has made known in Christ. Such a discernment will lead to both an affirmation of all that can be a *praeparatio evangelica* and to a setting aside of what is clearly contrary to God's will as it has been made known in Christ and made effective in the Church through the work of the Holy Spirit.

In the prophetic writings, a prominent model for describing how God is working out his universal plan is the *centripetal* model, where the nations all come to Mount Zion to participate in the Jewish cult and people request instruction of the Jews (Is. 2:1–4; Mic. 4:1–4; Zech. 8:20–23; 14:16–21, etc.). This has remained a way of witness for God's people, whether of the old or the new covenant: Come and see what the Lord is doing in our midst and be blessed by it.

The story of Jonah, however, presents another way: that of being *sent* (cf. Is. 6:8), a *centrifugal* model, if you like. Thus, in the

Servant Songs, the Servant brings justice to the nations, is a light to the Gentiles and the agent of God's law and of his salvation to the farthest corners of the earth (Is. 42:1–4; 49:6). *How* the Servant achieves this is another matter. It is not necessary to think of the Servant himself as a missionary to recognize the universal reach of his ministry. As we have seen, however, Jesus himself seems to have been aware from the beginning of the universal implications of his ministry and explicitly adduces the examples of Elijah being sent to the widow of Zarephath and of Elisha to Naaman as justifications for his own work (Lk. 4:24–27).

The book of Isaiah ends with a vision that combines a moving out by *Gentile* missionaries to declare the glory of God among the nations with the gathering in of the Diaspora as well as the 'nations and tongues'. Here both the centripetal and the centrifugal aspects of mission are held together in a tension that is almost unbearable but necessary, nevertheless. God's purposes in choosing Israel are now revealed to be the declaration of his glory throughout the world and the uniting of Jew and Gentile in a common worship of the God of Israel (Is. 66:8–23). Here is a vision that the Christian Church must own and that, by God's help, it seeks to fulfil so that all the barriers are broken down in Christ (Eph. 2:11–22) and there is 'neither Jew nor Greek, slave nor free, male nor female, for you are all one in Christ Jesus' (Gal. 3:28).

God's saving action in the world leads us to ask what sort of God this is, who saves in these ways, and how our understanding of God's revelation of himself can help us in a properly Christian assessment of peoples, cultures and religions. As ever, we find that a Trinitarian doctrine of God is essential here as, indeed, it is in our understanding of the human vocation and of human relationships, and also in matters of church order.[23]

If the Creator has made us in his own image, and made men and women together in his image and has given them a common task to be fulfilled in distinctive ways, it will be possible for human beings, even in their state of alienation and rebellion, to acknowledge this image in them, however partially, and to recognize their vocation, however imperfectly. Because the image has been corrupted and obscured by sin, it is an aspect of God's saving work to reveal what the image of God is really like. It is for this reason that the New Testament emphasizes that Jesus Christ, in his person and work, is the *eikōn* of God (2 Cor. 4:4; Col. 1:15), the exact representation (character) of God's being (Heb. 1:3). Such a revelation makes *anamnesis* possible. That is, by beholding Christ as the image of God, we are enabled to recall something of how we too are meant to be in God's image. Such an *anamnesis* can then lead to *metanoia* – to repentance and conversion – so that by joining ourselves to Christ we partake of the benefits of all he has done for us, and begin to recover the nature and calling of our original creation, which is to be in God's image and to be his stewards on earth (Gen. 1:26–28).

Even when God's image in us is corrupt and obscured, it is possible for human beings to know something of God's goodness and purpose because the image has not been wholly destroyed. Such a recognition can certainly allow, and even encourage, dialogue between Christians and others, even if, from the Christian point of view, the dialogue will have a dynamic that moves us to consider how God's image is fully revealed in Christ.

God's eternal Word and Wisdom, by whom we have been created (Ps. 33:6; Prov. 8:22–31; Wisdom 7; Jn. 1:1–3; Heb. 1:1–3), is incarnate in Jesus Christ and is also 'the true light, which enlightens everyone' (Jn. 1:9, NRSV). We have seen how the early Christian Apologists identify the Word and Wisdom of God with the *Logos* of the Stoics, the Divine Reason, which holds the universe together and provides order and stability for human society. The illumination of this Divine Reason can also be seen in the work of those who seek to understand more of the world in which we live and whose use of reason can be seen as a way of participating, even though partially, in the divine work. Although human creativity in art, poetry and prose is also affected by human fallenness, the early patristic writers, like St Paul before them, were, nevertheless, able to see the 'sparks of Divine Reason' here as well and thus to make connections with their pagan interlocuters.

Today, also, the illumination of the *Logos*, incarnate in Christ, can be the basis of conversations between Christians and others that lead towards the truth. Neither the idea of biblical Salvation-History and salvation-histories in general, nor that of the universal illumination of the *Logos* is necessarily, however, an endorsement of religious traditions, including their Christian manifestations. Salvation-histories may, indeed, be more clearly seen in *counter*-religious movements, such as those against the caste system in Hinduism or in the emphasis on the love of God in Sufism over and against legalistic understandings of Islam. For the early Fathers, certainly, the illumination of the *Logos* led, as often as not, to a critique of popular religion – and it can be the same today. I have tried, nevertheless, to show how the 'Christic' question is actually posed in different traditions. This may have to do with attempting to relate God to his world, or with the need for a mediator or even with the explicit acknowledgement of Jesus Christ in the renewal of a religious tradition. However, it is raised, it can provide a basis for dialogue.[24]

Fully forty years ago, my distinguished predecessor at CMS, John V. Taylor, drew our attention to the ubiquity of the Holy Spirit not only as the point of connection between God and human beings, but also as the medium in whom and through whom God communicates with us, and we with him and with another. The 'communion' or 'fellowship' of the Holy Spirit that we so often pray for in the grace (2 Cor. 13:14) is precisely what Taylor calls 'the in-between-ness' of the Holy Spirit. The Holy Spirit is the 'ground of our meeting', the one who makes communication possible at all.[25]

St John's Gospel speaks of the 'convincing' or 'convicting' work of the Spirit in the world. The Spirit convinces or convicts (*elenchein*) the world of sin, righteousness and judgement (16:8f.). This term is, on the one hand, related to the Socratic method of establishing truth through dialectic (question and answer) but, on the other hand, it is also related to the work of Hellenistic Jewish moralists such as Philo, who speak of the word of God acting upon the human conscience. The Spirit may then be thought of as acting on the world's conscience, showing the world its error and sin, the righteousness of Christ, by which alone we can be accounted righteous, and judgement for those who continue to reject the testimony of the Spirit, which is but a continuation of the testimony of Christ. It is important to distinguish here between those in the world who may be receptive to this work of the Spirit, however it is effected, whether through the witness of Christians or in some other way, and those who steadfastly refuse to receive this testimony (Jn. 14:17).

Metropolitan Georges Khodr of Mount Lebanon refers to the Orthodox doctrine of the economy of the Holy Spirit. According to him, the Spirit is present everywhere and fills everything. He points out that the Spirit is 'another Paraclete' (John 14:16) with a distinctive ministry, which is that of making Christ present and forming Christ within us. In this respect, he feels that certain aspects of other faiths may be seen as a response, even if partial, to the Spirit's work. These may have to do with how the truth is discerned in their scriptures, for example, or in the way certain individuals, and even movements, press on beyond the limits of a particular faith towards what he calls 'Christic values'.[26]

In a somewhat different way, Reformed traditions emphasize the prior work of the Holy Spirit in bringing about that renewal and recreation of the human personality that they speak of as conversion. This view is rooted in the Pauline (and Augustinian) tradition of fallen humanity's inability to free itself from the bondage of sin, and the need, therefore, of the prevenient work of the Spirit to renew and to bring to faith. Such a view clearly recognizes the sovereignty of the Spirit in the convicting and convincing work that leads to repentance, conversion and faith.

Metropolitan Khodr speaks of the economy of the Spirit as being distinct from that of the Son and calls this the 'hypostatic independence' of the Spirit. The advent of the Spirit in the world is not subordinated to the Son. It may be that here there is a reworking, in a new context, of the old debate between East and West as to whether the Spirit proceeds only from the Father or from the Father and the Son. Whatever the merits of the argument on either side, it is worth noting that Khodr also speaks of 'reciprocity' and 'mutual service' between the economies of the Son and of the Spirit. The dangers of tritheism are ever at the doors of Eastern Trinitarianism (just as those of modalism are for the Western version). A strong doctrine of *perichōrēsis* (the mutual indwelling and reciprocity of the three persons) is, therefore, essential if the unity of the Godhead is to be maintained.

It is true that the Spirit has a sphere of work that is peculiar to the Spirit: Pentecost is not merely a continuation of the incarnation but is its sequel or consequence, as Lossky has pointed out.[27] The Johannine witness is certainly of the freedom of the Spirit – the Spirit, like the wind, blows where it wishes and no one can predict what it will do – but that is not all that the Johannine tradition says of the Spirit. It also says that the Spirit is sent in the name of the Son and brings to remembrance all that the Son has said (Jn. 14:26). The Father sends the Spirit (14:16) but so does the Son (15:26), and the Spirit bears witness to Jesus. The Spirit does not speak on his own authority but delivers what is Christ's and glorifies him (16:13–15). Whatever else we may say of the economy of the Holy Spirit, Scripture is clear that the Spirit's work is to bear witness to God's revelation of himself in Jesus. We cannot, therefore, construct a theology of religions based on the economy of the Spirit that does not take this central fact into account.

The Pentecostal theologian, Amos Yong, has likewise pleaded for a Spirit-based theology of religions. He has noted how the experiences of the Spirit common among Pentecostals and charismatics have 'indubitable similarities' with the experiences of adherents of other traditions. For him, this opens up a way of exploring how the Spirit is present and active in other religions.[28] Well, maybe, but we ought to beware of two matters here: 'similarity' does not mean 'sameness'. What may appear as phenomenologically similar may, in fact, have very different origins. R.C. Zaehner's work on drug-induced mysticism and on the different kinds of mystical experience that exist even within particular religious traditions has shown how fraught this area is. We must not build our theologies of religion on sand![29]

How much can we say, then? We can gladly acknowledge the Spirit's work in the world and in the lives of individuals and communities, turning them towards God, who is their creator and who also desires their salvation. Signs of the Spirit's presence and work will be discerned in their consonance with the good news in Jesus Christ and also by the fruit in their lives of love, joy, peace, patience, gentleness, kindness, goodness and faithfulness (Gal. 5:22). In the same way, all that makes for impurity, licentiousness, idolatry, enmity, strife, jealousy, anger, selfishness, dissension, envy, drunkenness, etc. is clearly not of the Spirit (Gal. 5:19–21). To the extent, then, that the different religious communities reflect what we know to be God's will for us, as it has been revealed in Christ, we can say that the Spirit is working among them but always impelling them towards the fulfilment of all authentic spiritual aspirations in Christ (Eph. 1:10).

We have seen that there is an innate spiritual awareness in human beings, which moves them towards intimacy with the one who is the source of their existence. The human condition is not, however, as God willed it to be. It is affected also by human contrariness and rebelliousness, by a turning away from the source of all illumination and inspiration. Among other things, this produces bad, false and harmful forms of religious belief, which stand under judgement. God continues, nevertheless, to work for the fulfilment of his purposes in the lives of individuals and of nations.

We have tried to see how the Bible witnesses to this work of God and how the Trinity as a whole is involved in this project of salvation. In this context, we have sought to set out the principles and criteria by which Christians can understand and relate to other religious traditions and to their adherents. Such a way of relating will be full of confidence in the God who is both creator and saviour, but it will also be realistic about human sin and the distance this has created between God and humanity. Our approach will be sympathetic towards those whose condition we share but it will also be clear about how God has set about dealing with our alienation and waywardness. While we will take full account of the different human responses to the divine, we will continue to emphasize the priority of divine disclosure and of divine rescue. Any adequate response will have to be, by God's grace, a response to all that God has revealed and done in Christ.

6

The Unique and Universal Mission

We have seen who Jesus is and what he does. We have considered the implications of God's revelation of himself in Jesus for culture and for humanity's spiritual destiny. We have seen how the Holy Spirit continues to bear witness to Jesus and to be that medium in which the gospel can be both lived and communicated.

Recognizing, then, the absolute priority of the *Missio Dei*, the mission of the Trinitarian God, Father, Son and Holy Spirit, to the world, we have to ask about the Church's role in this mission. In the Pastoral Epistles, the Church is called the 'pillar and bulwark' of the truth (1 Tim. 3:15, NRSV) but it is also the agency by means of which the manifold wisdom of God is to be made known. The apostolic witness is placed firmly within this ecclesial reality (Eph. 3:7–13). The Great Commission, given to the Eleven in the first instance, also reflects the missionary nature and responsibility of the Church. The presence of the risen Christ in his Church is, then, quite intimately related to the continuing mission of the Church (Matthew 18:19–20).

The Church has fulfilled this task, badly or well, down the ages and in a number of ways. In this, it has been assisted or hindered by the movement of peoples, power relations between rulers, hospitality or hostility towards its missionaries and, of course, its own enthusiasms and limitations. Movements such as monasticism have arisen to recall the Church to fidelity and to renew it for its continuing task. Others, such as the great missionary societies, have sought to be a focus and a channel for what is really the responsibility of all.

What are the essential features, the 'marks', if you like, of the missionary obligation, which every Christian community, and the Church as a whole, need to have, to retain and, if necessary, to recover? What follows is a description of such characteristics. It is not exhaustive by any means and what is described here could also be put in other ways. If the Church were not committed to the nurture of some of these qualities, however, it would remain deficient in its understanding of mission and in its discharge of its missionary duties.

We have seen how the theme of 'sending' (*shālach*) is already emerging in the Older Testament. The prophets are sent with God's word to the people (Is. 6:8 is but one example of such a sending), the Servant is given a mission that extends to the farthest parts of the earth and to the nations (Is. 42:1–8; 49:6) and the missionaries from the nations go out to gather in both the children of Israel and the Gentiles so that they can worship God together (Is. 66:18–24).

It is in the New Testament, however, that the theme of 'sending' or 'being sent' or 'going' achieves a special prominence. When Jesus sends (*apostellein*) the Twelve on their mission of preaching, teaching and healing, he sends them to 'the lost sheep of the house of Israel' (Mt. 10:5ff. and parallels). It is well known that in Luke there is a report of another sending of the Seventy or Seventy-Two (10:1–12). Whichever number is preferred (the evidence seems evenly balanced), the suggestion appears to be that this sending prefigures the universal mission of the Church, which is to come after its Pentecostal birthday and is directed at the 70 (or, as the Septuagint has it, 72) nations that were thought to constitute the whole of humanity.[1]

Ananias was told in a vision that the erstwhile enemy of the Church was a chosen instrument who would carry the gospel to the nations (Acts 9:15). This sense of being sent is, of course, characteristic of St Paul in all his missionary journeys and labours. In his wonderfully prophetic book *Missionary Methods – St Paul's or Ours?*, the Anglican missionary-statesman Roland Allen emphasizes, first, the corporate nature of the conversion to which Paul was calling his Gentile audience. As we have seen, Paul's own apostolic task was placed squarely within the calling of the Church of God and he wanted to gather those who came to repentance and to faith in Christ into the society to which he belonged. Secondly, as we saw in Chapter 4, Allen shows that Paul did not seek to perpetuate dependence on the missionary and on missionary organizations among his converts. As Allen puts it crisply, 'He founded churches not missions.' Thirdly, Paul sought to provide all that such a church would need for its own spiritual health and for the continuation of mission in terms of ministry, sacraments, teaching and networks of fellowship.[2] If the witness of the Jewish synagogue in the Diaspora was largely a product of circumstances, whether of exile or of trade, the planting of churches in the Gentile world was a deliberate policy of mission.[3]

One of the objectives of Christian mission, then, must be the emergence of Christian communities in every locality so that effective Christian witness and service may be established among the people in each city, town or village. Such a commitment to *presence* is what lies behind the importance given in Christian history to territory. Churches in the New Testament are usually identified by the place in which they are located, whether Antioch, Ephesus, Corinth or Rome. This continues in the early patristic period with, perhaps, even more emphasis on locality (e.g. in the letters of Ignatius on his way to martyrdom) and is confirmed by the Canons of Nicaea.

The Church of England has for long held to an 'incarnational' view of its place in society. This has meant a commitment – sometimes a costly commitment in terms of property, finance and human resources – to maintaining a presence in every community in the land. All kinds of issues arise from such a commitment. One is the nature of Christian ministry. Whose responsibility is it to ensure that ancient Church buildings are kept in good repair – the Church or the State or a partnership between the two? And what is a viable Christian community in a particular place? The Church of England is not, of course, unique in this respect. All those Churches that may be called 'folk churches', for instance, the Scandinavian Lutherans or even the Church of Scotland, share this commitment to place. In some countries, the Roman Catholic Church may be the national Church, even if it has no official status, and it then displays some of the marks of a folk church as, indeed, do the Orthodox Churches.[4]

One of the questions that has arisen in connection with this territorial way of conceiving the Church is that today where people live is not as important for them as who they work with, play with and have common interests with. Networks, professional, social and recreational, are more and more important in people's lives and it is vital to ask how 'being church' can be expressed in the context of such networks. This is a move from merely planting churches in new areas to new ways of being church.[5]

The second question that has arisen regarding territoriality has to do with fidelity to the apostolic faith. What are Christians and Churches to do when the leadership of a particular church has significantly departed from the teaching of Scripture and biblical norms of faith and Christian living? Cyprian of Carthage is clear that communion is to be held only with orthodox bishops and their churches. Clergy and people cannot be held to communion with bishops who have compromised the faith. The so-called 'letters of communion' in the Early Church established not only the orthodoxy of the communicants, but also of the church from which they came. During the Arian controversy, the constant question was about bishops being in communion with one another. Where bishops had departed from the orthodox and catholic faith, orthodox bishops were often willing to provide episcopal oversight to those who remained faithful and even to ordain bishops for them. In Augustine's time, there were Donatist and Catholic bishops and churches in the same towns but not in communion with one another.

Contrary to what is often said, the dilemma was not so much about a 'sinless' or 'perfect' church as about persistent false teaching on any aspect of the faith, or persistent immorality that was not confessed and repented of but might even be justified on theological grounds. The situation in the Early Church seems to be a reflection of the biblical principle that systematic false teaching and persistent immorality can be reasons for a rupture in fellowship, even if it is temporary and orientated towards the restoration of those in error (1 Cor. 5:9–13; 2 Thes. 3:14–15; 2 Pet. 2:1–22; 2 Jn. 10; Jude 8–23, etc).[6] If and when such a rupture happens on a widespread scale (God forbid), the question is not about territory, buildings and the like but about which bishop, with clergy and the faithful, is in a particular place, holding to the essentials of the biblical and catholic faith or, where there is no such bishop, how faithful clergy and people may be provided with appropriate episcopal oversight.

The presence of the Church in a particular place or among a specific group of people can be alienating. It can be, and has been at different periods in history, associated with the forces of oppression, occupation or violence. It is important, therefore, to stress that authentic presence, if it is to be truly incarnational, must be one that identifies with the culture, aspirations and perceived destiny of a people, as far as this is possible without compromising the nature of the gospel.

At the same time, however, the Church must constantly guard against the danger of simply capitulating to culture and being incorporated into the spirit of the age. Along with the commitment to presence and to identification, then, there also has to be a commitment to the prophetic, a willingness to stand over and against the culture, system of belief and way of life of a particular people in order to uphold the gospel and its values. There is always a temptation to submit to being co-opted into a system in the hope of obtaining privilege and 'influence'. But the consequence is that the Church can no longer speak from the cutting-edge on what the gospel has to say about dignity, liberty, justice and the common good.

The Church has both a glorious history of martyrdom for the sake of Christ and his kingdom and also a somewhat grubby past of compromise with those who want Christianity to be 'respectable' and not to challenge the accepted order. In recent years there has been a willingness to widen the category of martyrs to include not only those who died because of *odium fidei*, that is, because of a specific hatred of the faith, but also those who died to protect the life of another (such as Maximilian Kolbe) or for the sake of justice in society (such as Oscar

Romero). By their deaths, they are seen as witnesses to Christian love and to God's demand for justice.[7]

Such a widening of the understanding of martyrdom in the Christian tradition is seen most clearly in the ten statues of modern martyrs, which were dedicated in 1998 and occupy niches in the façade of the west front of Westminster Abbey – one of the best-known views in the world. As well as Maximilian Kolbe and Oscar Romero, the list includes the Pakistani evangelist Esther John, who was killed by a Muslim extremist, Janani Luwum, Archbishop of Uganda, murdered for resisting Idi Amin and Wang Zhi Ming, a Chinese pastor killed during the cultural revolution in China. In his introduction to the brochure issued for the dedication, Anthony Harvey, then Sub-Dean of the Abbey has this to say:

> The ten statues are of individual martyrs; but they are intended to represent all those others who have died (and continue to die) in similar circumstances of oppression and persecution . . . They include victims of the struggle for human rights in North and South America, of the Soviet and Nazi persecution in Europe, of religious prejudice and dictatorial rule in Africa, of fanaticism in the Indian sub-continent, of the brutalities of the Second World War in Asia and of the Cultural Revolution in China . . . thousands of men and women have paid with their lives for their faith and their convictions.[8]

Rahner's suggestion that the category of martyr should be widened to include those who are engaged in struggle out of the depths of their Christian conviction is based on a view of the work of Jesus himself as a struggle for truth, and opposition to those who would deny people access to God, freedom to be what God intended them to be, and the justice that allows their basic needs to be met. According to Rahner, it was this struggle that led to the death of Jesus. His patient endurance of suffering and death cannot be separated from his life of struggle.[9] In this connection, it is worth noting that half of the ten commemorated on the west front of the Abbey are those whose lives were marked by active Christian witness.

This brings us to a dimension of Christian mission that can be called *action*. From the earliest days, Christians were known to be active in their generosity and involvement with the needy. As Peter Phan has said, the early Church continued to grow rapidly, in spite of bloody persecutions and internal divisions, partly because of its sense of community, its willingness to aid those in need, whether Christian or pagan, and its insistence on biblically-derived social duties.[10] E. A. Judge, the Australian scholar, remarks, '[Early Christianity was about] the deliberate abandonment of status so as to open the way to a new spirit of human co-operation through mutual service.' This character-istic mutuality has also been noticed by New Testament scholars such as Charlie Moule as underlying, for example, the house-hold codes in Ephesians and Colossians and as providing what was distinctively Christian in this area of ethical thought.[11] The discipline of biblical sociology has noticed the egalitarian and inclusive nature of the early Christian communities and this was, surely, a major cause of their rapid expansion in class-ridden societies.[12]

In their preaching and writing, the early Fathers were assiduous in encouraging active Christian service towards the poor, the sick, the imprisoned and strangers. It may well have been the case that for many this was a first point of contact with the Christian faith. The Cappadocian Gregory of Nazianzus' homily, *Love of the Poor*, is a good example of such teaching. By the 'poor' Gregory means anyone in need and all those who suffer unjustly. Private property is, strictly speaking, a matter of stewardship of the resources we have been allocated by Providence and sharing is an obligation. Our love of the poor is based on the fact that we share a common humanity with them.

The sheer amount of John Chrysostom's preaching and teach-ing on social questions marks him out for special treatment. Once again, John emphasizes solidarity in our common human-ity as a reason for sharing the good things of life. The very purpose of having possessions is to share them. He has a positive view of work and points out that in a just society work would be orientated towards what is useful and necessary rather than towards providing luxuries and catering for vices. He is concerned not only with the private charity of Christians, but also with the corporate work of the Church – with widows, those in prisons and hospitals, those ill at home, the maimed, strangers and the indigent. According to him, both Christians and the Church as a whole are made most Christ-like when they care for their neighbour.[13]

With such a strong social tradition in the East, it is no accident that various kinds of almshouses to care for widows, orphans, the poor and the sick spread, like monasticism itself, from the East to Western Christendom. These were, in due course, to form the foundations for hospitals as we know them. Education was also a fruit of the monastic movement. Monasteries housed libraries and archives; they were the publishing houses of the Middle Ages. Bishops and cathedrals also had schools where scholars could be found. Such intellectual activity eventually gave rise to the university and to organized and systematic study of a number of disciplines, theology remaining, of course, the queen of the sciences.[14]

The Renaissance and the Reformation did not interfere with the development of medical and other institutions in the west, though this sometimes became more secular, with rulers, cities and voluntary organizations providing for new foundations. The Evangelical Revival in Britain in the eighteenth century, however, led to a new concern for the industrial poor, for the education of poor children and, of course, for the ending of the slave trade and the emancipation of slaves. The leaders of this revival, for instance, the members of the Clapham Sect, were also committed to taking the gospel to the farthest corners of the world. Indeed, some of their social concern arose out of their commitment to mission.[15]

As Bebbington has shown, most evangelicals in the eighteenth and early nineteenth centuries were postmillennialists, that is to say, they believed that an era of peace and prosperity would be ushered in by the preaching of the gospel throughout the world and then Christ would come to claim his kingdom. This belief was, however, gradually replaced by premillennialism, which held that Christ would come first and would then usher in his kingdom. This premillennialism was, moreover, often accompanied by Adventism, which encouraged eager expectation of an imminent return. These currents in evangelicalism led to a withdrawal from worldly concerns to introversion and to forms of pietism.

In the 1960s and 1970s, evangelical quietism began to be challenged from the inside. World poverty was one of the elements that impinged on the Christian conscience and a range of agencies came into existence to facilitate Christian involvement in this area. Through the work of David Sheppard, Alan Storkey and others, Christians were also being sensitized to multiple deprivation in the inner cities. It was, however, at the Lausanne Congress of 1974 that repentance was expressed for recent evangelical neglect of social responsibility and a follow-up conference declared that evangelism and social responsibility, while distinct from one another, were integrally related in our proclamation of the gospel and our obedience to it.[16]

Networks of Christian leaders, pastors, theologians, missionaries and development workers began to form organizations such as Partnership in Mission Asia, the Latin American Theological Fraternity, and the African Theological Fraternity, all later to be brought together under the umbrella of the International Fellowship of Evangelical Mission Theologians. One of the aims of these networks was to develop a holistic view of mission, variously termed 'integral evangelism', 'mission as transformation' or 'integral mission'. By these terms, their users meant an understanding of mission and evangelism that brings together proclamation of the gospel and seeking repentance and conversion, with involvement in action for justice and seeking to bring social transformation to structures and communities.[17]

It is perhaps worth pointing out that although the Lausanne movement agreed about the twin imperatives of evangelism and social responsibility, there was less agreement on whether such responsibility included social action to challenge injustice and oppression and whether churches, as opposed to individuals and groups of Christians, would engage in such action. While many would have been content with social service, bodies like INFEMIT (the International Fellowship of Evangelical Mission Theologians) promoted active involvement of both individuals and churches in movements to empower the poor.[18]

It should also be remembered that in the ecumenical movement, the methods promoted by the Life and Work Movement and by William Temple's Conference on Politics, Economics and Citizenship were those of divergent Christians and Christian traditions coming to a common mind on the complex issues facing humanity and, particularly, the poor and the disadvantaged. From the 1960s onwards they began to be criticized as abstract and top down, framed by people who were comfortable with the powers that be, even if they sought to influence them with Christian ideals. Instead, Christians, especially from Africa, Asia and Latin America, began to commend 'direct action' in terms of participation in social struggle to serve justice in society. Some programmes of the World Council of Churches began to reflect this approach. The well-known Programme to Combat Racism (PCR) and the Commission for the Churches' Participation in Development (CCPD), for instance, were founded on the principle that solidarity has to be expressed with the poor and their side has to be taken in the conflict that must precede the securing of justice for them. It is interesting to see how in both recent evangelicalism and in the ecumenical movement there have been moves away from social teaching and service to social action with direct social, economic and political objectives and consequences.[19]

The Second Vatican Council unleashed forces in the Roman Catholic Church that brought about, among many other movements, the emergence of liberation theology. This is not the place to recount the history or to assess the theology and political orientations of this movement. We need, however, to notice two aspects that are closely related but are often viewed and treated separately.

The basic ecclesial communities, which emerged after the Council and were based on and gave rise to the characteristic insights of liberation theology, originated in a dynamic to express and to reform the Church so that it was genuinely *community* rather than being merely a hierarchical structure. In the absence of a priest, they enabled the people to gather, to praise and celebrate together, to reflect on God's Word, to pray for the needs of those around them and even to celebrate the Lord's Supper, which could not, of course, be a celebration of the Mass but was, nevertheless, a way of communicating with the crucified, risen and ascended Lord.

All sorts of ecclesiological questions can be and are asked about these communities but we are bound to note the close relationship between community and worship. The prayer of the community for those in need, moreover, leads to an advocacy of such people in wider society and, where there is resistance to justice and compassion, to action in the political arena. Prayer, service, advocacy and struggle are all integrated in the life and mission of such a community.[20]

It is paradoxical, therefore, that it should be the failure to give adequate attention to spirituality in the base communities movement that has resulted in the huge popularity of Pentecostal options in Latin America. What could not be achieved through political struggle is being achieved by changed lives, which the Pentecostals emphasize, and this is resulting in stronger families, reliable workers, who are then rewarded by their employers, the virtues of saving, and better education and housing. There are certainly lessons here for the Roman Catholic Church but not for this Church alone.[21]

In the previous chapter, we considered briefly the biblical and Trinitarian basis of a properly Christian assessment of religious traditions, including, of course, Christian versions of these traditions. We also saw, however, how the Bible and our doctrine of God can provide us with the resources for dialogue with people of different faith. We now need to notice that dialogue is not just about religious traditions. Language and, therefore, conversation are intrinsic to human nature. It is possible, moreover, for human beings to transcend their own world of discourse and at least to try to enter, even if temporarily, the worlds of others. Christian missionaries should always be aware of the importance of crossing language, cultural and other barriers – only thus can the gospel be communicated across cultures whether these are far away or near at hand.[22]

Dialogue, then, should be about the whole of life. It should take account not only of people's beliefs and world views, but also of their social, economic and political circumstances. There are many kinds of dialogue and each has a particular form that is suited to its own purpose. There is, for example, the dialogue where the primary purpose is for the partners to learn from one another. This may be about the doctrines and beliefs of another religious tradition or, more generally, it may be about cultural norms such as food, dress, the place of women and men in society, forms of governance and so on, all of which are often informed by religious belief. It should be noted that each partner in the dialogue is committed to their view and that this is to be respected. If, however, such dialogue is not to become a 'set piece' where those taking part do little more than exchange notes about one another, then it is important that as well as a recognition of what is held in common and areas where there is a convergence of views, there should also be mutual challenge and debate.

Another kind of dialogue focuses not so much on an exchange of information as on the nature of the spiritual life and how each partner is nurtured in this life by their tradition. While needing to be aware that human beings have a common spiritual nature, and recognizing their deepest aspirations, we should beware of false notions of the 'oneness' of spiritual or mystical experience. We have seen in Chapter 5 how mystical experiences that appear phenomenologically similar may have very different origins indeed. We should also not forget that spiritual experiences are, and have to be, evaluated within particular traditions, theological, psychological and philosophical.

A form of dialogue that is assuming greater significance today has to do with the building up of community. Integration does not necessarily mean assimilation. The culture and beliefs of individuals and groups should be respected but a common language is also necessary if social, economic and political life is to be effective. There has to be some identification of the values by which a particular community lives and some commitment on the part of others, both individuals and groups, to own such values in their common life. Dialogue is an essential aspect of promoting proper integration.

Then there is the dialogue that is about identifying and being committed to fundamental human freedoms, such as freedom of expression, of belief (including changing one's belief), of worship, of family life, etc. Dialogue enables partners to recognize the problems that may exist in a particular part of the world or in the context of a specific religious tradition, and to find solutions that are grounded in the tradition of each. Once again, there is an urgent need for such dialogue today.[23]

We have seen how terms such as *dialegomai* and *dialogizomai* are used in the New Testament to mean discussion or argument conducted for the sake of persuasion. This was also the way in which such terms were used in Christian antiquity from Justin Martyr in the second century to St John of Damascus in the eighth. In philosophy too the terms often refer to the Socratic method, that is, a dialectical way of arriving at the truth.

In the Christian use of the term 'dialogue', therefore, there has always been an element of witness and of persuasion. It was not until modern times that some ecumenically-minded Christians began to question the validity and the permissibility of witness in the context of dialogue. In the documents of the ecumenical movement there has been some ambivalence on this issue. There is, however, no need for this. Authentic dialogue cannot take place unless and until those involved are prepared to lay bare the wellsprings of their motivation to engage in dialogue at all. There can be no coercion, of course, nor should there be any manipulation, but dialogue would be meaningless unless we were able, with sensitivity and love, to bear witness to all that Christ means to us, what he has done for us and what he longs to do for our partners in dialogue. It goes without saying that our readiness to witness must also be accompanied by our readiness to listen to our partners with utmost attention and with the greatest respect as they too reveal what motivates them towards dialogue.[24]

Dialogue can take place in highly structured situations, such as the dialogue between Al-Azhar, the premier place of Sunni learning, located in Cairo, and the Roman Catholic Church or the Anglican communion. There can be the dialogue of scholars such as the dialogue I helped George Carey, then Archbishop of Canterbury, and Prime Minister Tony Blair to initiate after the tragedy of the terrorist attacks on 9/11. As we have seen, there can also be dialogue between those who seek to understand the spiritual experience of the other. Dialogue between those of the 'religious life' in different faith traditions has often been of this sort. Most important, of course, is what the Vatican has called 'the dialogue of life', that is to say, the daily conversation and mutual learning that goes on among neighbours, colleagues at work or study, and even family members. Dialogue at every level has its own justification and it is not necessary to sacrifice one for the sake of the other. Rather, they need to be held together so that their cumulative benefit can be experienced by individuals, communities, nations and even internationally.[25]

Christian presence is for the sake of witness. We seek to identify with people's hopes and fears, with their culture and idiom, so that we can, in word and deed, give an account of the hope that is in us (1 Pet. 3:15), point people to Christ and ask them to put their trust in him as we can testify to having done ourselves. The martyrs are witnesses of a special kind; by their testimony they reignite the fire in us. Evangelism and social responsibility are, as we have seen, 'like the two blades of a pair of scissors' or 'the two wings of a bird'[26] and dialogue can be the setting for 'authentic witness'.

In their commitment to the wholeness of mission, and to its integrity, the Church and Christians will be aware that in the course of our presence among people, in our friendship with them and our service for them, there will be opportunities for sharing the good news of Jesus. These may arise at times of joy or sorrow, at important milestones in people's lives or when it is demanded by the depth of friendship itself. Evangelism (or, if you prefer, evangelization, suggesting more of a process than an event) is both a necessary aspect of mission and its crown because in the course of it we are pointing beyond ourselves to the one who is the source of our missionary involvement.

One of the reasons for preaching the gospel is that Christ, who is the image of the invisible God, reminds us that we too have been made in the divine image. In Chapter 5, we saw how this theme of *anamnesis* is important in our understanding of the human response to the call of God in the proclamation of the gospel. In the Platonic dialogues, *anamnesis* is about the recovery of fundamental knowledge of ourselves as human beings. In the Bible also, in both the Older and the New Testaments, there is considerable emphasis on remembering

God's righteousness, his loving kindness, his covenant and his commandments. It is, however, in the Parable of the Prodigal in Luke 15 that this sense of *anamnesis* comes to the fore.

In verse 17 of Luke 15, we are told that as a result of his privations, the son 'came to himself' or 'came to his senses' (*eis heauton erchesthai*). Kenneth Bailey, with his eye, as ever, on the oriental background, points out that the Syriac translations have 'he came to his *nefesh*' (he came back to his own self) and that the medieval Arabic translations and commentaries agree.[27] The son recalled what he had been and saw what he had become. This is the beginning, perhaps, of repentance, but not its climax. Here is the acknowledgement that he has 'sinned' and is not worthy of returning to his father's house as a son. According to the Arab commentators, it is not until the demonstration of the father's unconditional love that the repentance becomes complete. Now he is not simply wanting to serve out his penance in servitude but is willing to be restored as a son: *anamnesis* then leads to *metanoia*, to that complete turning around towards God, his grace and his love, which make new life possible for us. As with the Prodigal, this is a restoration to what we were always intended to be but it is also a fresh start. It is the beginning of a transformation that must start with the person but has ever deepening and ever widening effects in those around and in the world generally.

Along with the late Sir Norman Anderson, we can say that because of the Holy Spirit's prevenient work, many who are outside the reach of the Church can be 'brought back to themselves' and can throw themselves on God's mercy. It is then the task of evangelism to bring to them the Father's unconditional love and the assurance of forgiveness. Even if that does not happen, Sir Norman believes that God in Christ will be revealed to them somehow and that they will receive mercy and come to worship their Saviour on both this side of the grave and on the other. We need not speculate on how this might happen but leave it to God's gracious sovereignty. It is important here to note that Sir Norman is not saying that people can be saved by their beliefs or by the religious systems to which they belong but by invoking that mercy and love of God that, as Christians, we know to have been most fully revealed for our sakes in the cross of Christ. He is saying that those who ask for such mercy will not be denied it.[28]

That, of course, leaves the question of assurance hanging in the air. After all, it is important not only that we realize how miserable we are as sinners and how much we need God's mercy, but also that we have, indeed, been rescued by him and made to sit with Christ in the heavenly places (Eph. 2:6). Again, this is a reason for evangelism: people need to know that in Christ a suffering God has dealt with that alienation from the source of our being that is the root cause of our suffering and that of the world around us (Rom. 8:18–25). The cross reveals God's love to us but also shows us that we are worthy of love. Assurance is about the significance of human life created and redeemed by God. It leads to confidence in our destiny as beings destined for eternal fellowship with God, who has, at great cost, made this fellowship possible again.[29] It is about putting our whole trust in the Good Shepherd, who has assured us that he will never drive away anyone who comes to him, that he will never lose anyone in his care and that he will raise us up at the last day (John 6:35–40; 10:4,9,14–16; Rom 10:9). Assurance is both about the certainty of revealed truth and also about our investment in it. In classical Christian theology, an inward sense of assurance must be accompanied by right belief, love of fellow Christians and right conduct (this is, in fact, the burden of 1 John).

True evangelism, then, is not just about making people aware of their shortcomings and bringing them to repentance, but it is also about that assurance that springs from faith in what God has revealed, and trust in the one who has given us this knowledge of his purpose for us.

The gospel is not only the reason for a 'turning about' and a 'beginning again', it is also about the fulfilment of a person's or even a group's deepest spiritual aspirations. Because human beings have been made in the divine image, there is a restlessness and a hunger in every human heart for God. Human cultures and even religious traditions can display not only aspirations for a restored fellowship with God, but also anticipations, dimmer or fuller, of the good news in Christ. Once again, evangelism brings people to this kind of fulfilment or *anakephalaiōsis* in Christ. Nor can we leave it at individual fulfilment. As we have seen, this can also be about the fulfilment of the deepest aspirations found in cultures and of the noblest ideals even in religious traditions. Indeed, in Ephesians and in St Irenaeus, it is nothing less than the fulfilment of all the authentic hopes and aspirations of all of history. Not only that, it is also about the ultimate destiny of the universe itself (Eph. 1:10).[30]

Evangelism is truly educational in the sense that it brings out what is deeply implanted in the soul or, to change the metaphor, by it, as numerous mystics have recognized, the rusty mirror of the heart is polished up again so that it can reflect that divine image so completely revealed in Christ. Evangelism is not the whole of mission but without it our mission is not complete. If it is thought of as a process – evangelization – then we can think of it as directed both outwards and inwards. Even as the Church takes the gospel to the world, it is also continuously being evangelized by it (e.g. Eph. 3:1–20). Those who bring the good news to others need also to be continuously shaped by it lest, as St Paul says, having preached to others, they themselves should be found unacceptable (1 Cor. 9:23–27).[31]

So far we have concentrated on the conversion of an individual or, perhaps, of groups, but the question has been raised about the possibility of the conversion to Christ of whole religious traditions. We have seen already, in Chapter 2, how different faith traditions have been affected by the influence of Christ on them. In systems such as Hinduism it is not an exaggeration to say that views of divinity, the estimate of human dignity and social teaching have been transformed by the encounter, not so much with Christian missionary work, as with Christ himself. *Mutatis mutandis*, this can be said of other traditions as well.

For many years, John V. Taylor has argued for the possibility of the conversion of religious traditions to Christ. For him, all such traditions are partial and, in some respects, even erroneous responses to the work of the Holy Spirit. The coming of Christ to such traditions is, of course, judgement but it can also be fulfilment in that the true object of their response is revealed. What is true in them will be completed, error will be exposed and corrected, disobedience turned to obedience and an intimate worship of God renewed. It is to be noted that Taylor places historic Christianity within the religious traditions needing conversion to Christ.[32]

Bishop Kenneth Cragg, in his long and distinguished interlocution with Islam, has sought to commend the gospel in terms of the logic of Islam itself. It is the truth of 'God in Christ' that is to be commended and that persuades people, at least partly, on the basis of what they know already from within their own tradition. In conversion, therefore, a recognition of, and an allegiance to, the gospel brings about both continuity with what has gone before and also discontinuity.[33]

Cragg and Taylor are such important students of spiritual traditions that we dare not neglect the significance of what they are saying. They are only too well aware of the obstacles in the way of a Christ-centred transformation. In some traditions, an acknowledgement of the transcendent does not at all involve a belief in a Supreme Being who acts savingly. In others, there are 'gods many and lords many' (1Cor. 8:5) and in yet others, God sends his messengers but the logic of divine compassion is not followed through and God does not come himself nor is he thought of as capable of suffering so that we may be reconciled to him. If the theology is hugely divergent, so is the anthropology: some deny the reality of personhood altogether, others affirm only its reality and destiny, while yet others deny that humanity is caught in a corporate web of its own wrongdoing from which it needs rescue.

Sensitive conveyors of the good news in every context will seek to make connections with the truth people know already, however partial that may be from the Christian point of view. They will seek also to influence culture, the political and economic order and even the religious tradition so that these approximate more and more to the will of God for creation and become more and more open to the good news of the redemption won for us by Christ. They will also be realistic enough to know that the gospel will challenge and change, whether that be individuals, communities or spiritual traditions. They will seek authentic transformation at every level but without compromising the essential core of the good news that in Christ God is, through costly self-sacrifice, reconnecting the world to himself (2 Cor. 5:19).

It seems to be the case that many religious traditions have been, and are being, powerfully affected by the figure of Jesus Christ. From the Christian point of view, the results of this are both positive and negative. With every advance there are regressions and withdrawals out of fear of what Christ might mean and the changes that would be necessary. It is difficult to see how systems founded on a denial of the Creator or of incarnation and atonement could be entirely transformed from the inside. We believe in a God of miracles, however, and if he can change people and cultures, there is no reason why the 'conversion to Christ' looked for by Taylor and Cragg should not take place in God's own time and in the light of his own saving purposes.

In the chapter on culture, we saw how there are some who are pressing the question as to how people can not only be brought to faith in the context of a particular culture, but also how they can continue to be disciples within a specific cultural framework. There are some among them who would take this further and ask how people can come to faith and be disciples of Jesus *within a non-Christian tradition of faith*. I have myself known those who would describe themselves as 'Hindu followers of Christ' and even 'Muslim followers'. What they mean by such terminology varies enormously and the implications for the cause of the gospel and for the Christian Church are immense.

Stanley Samartha describes one such 'Hindu follower of Christ'. Kalagora Subba Rao was a teacher and lecturer who was greatly revered for his work. Rao had a vision of Christ that changed his life dramatically and resulted in a ministry of healing in Christ's name (cf. Lk. 9:49–50). He had an intense devotion to Christ but consistently refused baptism and membership of any church. For Samartha, Subba Rao is undoubtedly Christocentric but within a Vedantic framework. Salvation continues to be understood in a Hindu way as freedom from illusion and Christ is the guru who shows the way. It may be that here we have an authentic Indian theology in the making and we should not make premature judgements on it. Some serious questions have to be raised, nevertheless, about the uniqueness of Christ and our relationship with him, the scheme of salvation and the place of the Church in such a scheme. We can understand Subba Rao's criticism of the Church and we can acknowledge its failures, but will his movement produce anything better? How will his teaching and, eventually, that of his followers, be related to the Church's witness down the ages and across the world?[34] Of course, not all 'Hindu Christians' are so radical. Dr Paul Sudhakar, for example, certainly describes himself in these terms but has at the same time made a notable contribution to the evangelical student movement in India.

Phil Parshall is an American missionary and missiologist who has for long been interested in the question of how Muslims who come to faith in Christ are to live in their culture. He has strongly criticized the tendency by missionaries and churches to 'extract' such people from their cultural setting and to transplant them into traditional 'Christian' cultures where they rapidly become misfits. He is a strong advocate of believers from Muslim backgrounds forming their own churches where they can worship, learn and live the life of a disciple of Christ in culturally appropriate ways.[35]

Mazhar Mallouhi is a believer with a Syrian Muslim background. At first, he attempted to integrate with Arab Christians but found that he was always under suspicion and was being asked to give up too much of his cultural and spiritual heritage. He has since been extremely creative in expressing his faith in terms that resonate with Muslims. In particular, he has specialized in reading the Bible with Muslim eyes and has published, for example, an Eastern reading of St Luke's Gospel and a Sufi reading of St John.[36]

While pilgrimages such as the ones described above are to be respected and even, perhaps, to be seen as providential in bridging the gulfs between different faiths, some questions remain, nevertheless. How will lone converts survive without a fellowship to sustain them when they experience hostility, opposition and even violence because of their following of Jesus? Again, while we can be sympathetic to people from a particular background coming together as a homogeneous expression of 'church', we have to ask how they are also related to the wider, heterogeneous Church so that they may be nurtured by both 'sameness' and 'difference' in the Body of Christ. Not only that, the whole Church needs their testimony and, indeed, their challenge if it is to transcend the parochial mindset that inevitably overcomes most Christian communities.

How far believers in Christ can continue to identify with the religious background from which they come depends on a number of factors. There are, first of all, the questions of compatibility between their faith and the tradition from which they come. Even Parshall has to admit discomfort as he attempted to join in the Muslim ritual prayer (the *Salāt*) and tells us that he will never again make such an attempt. He recognizes also the Qur'ānic rejection of central Christian doctrines, and while he acknowledges Muhammad, the Prophet of Islam, as an important reformer and leader, he cannot ascribe to him the titles that Muslims habitually give him.[37]

There is also the question of acceptance: will Muslims see the participation of a believer in their feasts, fasts and rituals as a form of deception that makes the apostasy worse? Parshall himself notes the fate of such Islamic groups as the *Ahmadiyya* and, surely, this should be a warning to us that orthodox Islam will not accept any deviation from its creed and certainly not the kind that Muslim background believers would bring to the fore.[38]

Believers will have to live and behave with integrity and loyalty. They cannot deny their experience, they cannot forsake their Lord. No accommodation is possible that asks them to speak or pray or act in a way that even implies such denial. They must, moreover, express solidarity with their brothers and sisters in Christ, however different their background. Once again, this cannot go hand in hand with the practice of the cult of another faith.

So what, then, is possible? It is possible for such believers to continue to practise the cultural norms of the community around them in terms of diet, clothing, habits of hygiene, etc. They can seek to express their faith in terminology drawn from the spiritual tradition around them, though with the provisos that such terminology does not compromise the essentials of the gospel and that it has the capacity for distinctive Christian content. Styles of worship – of posture, of singing and of architecture – can all be drawn from the culture and even the religious culture around them, provided that they have been tested and purified. As with Paul Sudhakar and Mazhar Mallouhi, a personal and deep knowledge of another religious tradition can certainly facilitate the communication of the good news of Jesus Christ to those who belong to such a tradition in a way that is fresh and has resonances with their spiritual background. Naturally, this has to be done with complete integrity, without distorting the gospel or misrepresenting the other tradition.

All of this is a formidable agenda but necessary for mission that is sensitive and respectful but also firm and distinctive. In mission strategy, there is no need to go after fads that lead nowhere, or to follow fashions in missiological thinking that may have the effect of compromising either the uniqueness or the universality of Christ or both. It is possible to be committed and creative in our missionary approach while at the same time being clear about how God has revealed himself in Jesus Christ, how through his sacrificial death he has set us right with him and how the resurrection of Jesus not only casts a new light on the whole of creation, but is also transforming it according to God's purpose, beginning with us.

The missionary task of the Church is multifaceted and enduring. Our approach must be to the whole person and the whole community for the sake of that wholeness that is God's will for his creation. We should pray earnestly for wisdom that we may not forget any part of our mandate and that through our thought and work the one God, Father, Son and Holy Spirit, may be glorified.

Notes

By Way of Introduction

1   On this last, see the report by the Mission Theological
     Advisory Group of the Church of England, *The Search for
     Faith and the Witness of the Church* (London: Church House
     Publishing, 1996).

1   Fundamental Values and Jesus of Nazareth

1   See further, Michael Nazir-Ali, 'Thinking and Acting
     Morally', *Crucible* (October–December 2002), 229f.

2   Colin Chapman, *Islam and the West* (Carlisle: Paternoster,
     1998), 123ff.

3   On this issue, see Nigel Biggar, *Aiming to Kill: The Ethics of
     Suicide and Euthanasia* (London: Darton, Longman & Todd,
     2004).

4   There is a huge literature on these matters but see *Personal
     Origins: The Report of a Working Party on Human Fertilisation
     and Embryology of the Board of Social Responsibility* (London:
     Church House Publishing, 1996), 38ff.; *Pre-conceived Ideas: A
     Christian Perspective of IVF and Embryology by the Church of
     Scotland Board of Social Responsibility* (Edinburgh: St Andrew
     Press, 1996), 50ff.; Robert Song, *Human Genetics: Fabricating
     the Future* (London: Darton, Longman & Todd, 2002), 33ff.;
     Francis George, 'The Need for Bioethical Vision' in John F.
     Kilner, C. Christopher Hook and Diann B. Uustal (eds.),

Cutting Edge Bioethics: A Christian Exploration of Technologies and Trends (Grand Rapids: Eerdmans, 2002), 90ff.

5   On this, see Richard Koch and Chris Smith, *Suicide of the West* (London and New York: Continuum, 2006).

6   On this, see further, Oliver O'Donovan, *Resurrection and Moral Order: An Outline for Evangelical Ethics* (Leicester: Inter-Varsity Press, 1986).

7   See further, Kevin Ward and Brian Stanley (eds.), *The Church Mission Society and World Christianity 1799–1999* (Richmond: Curzon Press and Grand Rapids: Eerdmans, 2000), 21f.

8   For an example, see Vinay Samuel and Chris Sugden (eds.), *Mission as Transformation: A Theology of the Whole Gospel* (Oxford: Regnum, 1999).

9   For how this has happened with Pentecostal Mission, see David Martin, *Pentecostalism: The World Their Parish* (Oxford: Blackwell, 2002).

10   See further, Michael Nazir-Ali, *Conviction and Conflict: Islam, Christianity and World Order* (London and New York: Continuum, 2006), 112ff.

11   William G. Young, *Patriarch, Shah and Caliph: A study of the relationship of the Church of the East with the Sassanid Empire and the early caliphates up to 820 A.D.* (Rawalpindi: Christian Study Centre, 1974), 21ff.

12   On the consequences of the Radical Reformation, see Owen Chadwick, *The Reformation* (London: Penguin, 1990), 188ff.

13   In the *Khaleej Times*, Friday, 9 January 1998, 5.

14   *Dignitatis Humanae*, 1965, 1:2 in Austin Flannery (ed.), *Vatican Council II: Conciliar and Post Conciliar Documents*, vol. I (Northport, N.Y.: Costello, 1988, rev. edn.), 801.

15   T.M. Greene and H.H. Hudson's introduction to Kant's *Religion within the Limits of Reason Alone* (New York: Harper, 1960), liff.

16   Joan O'Donovan, 'The Concept of Rights in Christian Moral Discourse' in Michael Cromartie (ed.), *A Preserving Grace: Protestants, Catholics and Natural Law* (Grand Rapids: Eerdmans/EPPC, 1997), 143ff. See also Robert George's reply in the same collection, 157f.

17   Alasdair MacIntyre, *After Virtue: A Study in Moral Theory* (London: Duckworth, 2000), 126ff., 256ff.

18 On this, see Thomas Cahill, *The Gifts of the Jews: How a Tribe of Desert Nomads Changed the Way Everyone Thinks and Feels* (Oxford: Lion, 1998).

19 See Michael Nazir-Ali, *Conviction and Conflict*, 54f.

20 See further, Rick Warren, *The Purpose-Driven Life: What on Earth Am I Here For?* (Grand Rapids: Zondervan, 2002).

21 For David Daniell on William Tyndale's contribution to the development of the English language, see his edition of *The Obedience of a Christian Man* (London: Penguin, 2000) xiiif., and *Selected Writings* (Manchester: Carcanet, 2003), viiff.

22 Greene and Hudson, *Religion within the Limits of Reason Alone*, 60ff., 95ff.

23 See the Mission Theological Advisory Group Report, *The Search for Faith*, especially 74ff.

24 On this issue, see Tariq Modood (ed.), *Church, State and Religious Minorities* (London: Policy Studies Institute, 1997).

25 John Habgood, *Confessions of a Conservative Liberal* (London: SPCK, 1988), 7ff.

26 Martin E. Marty, *When Faiths Collide* (Oxford: Blackwell, 2005).

27 See further, the Church of England report *Towards a Theology for Inter-faith Dialogue: Report of the Inter-faith Consultative Group of the Board for Mission and Unity* (London: Church Information Office, 1984), 9ff.

28 See on this, George Weigel, *The Cube and the Cathedral: Europe, America and Politics Without God* (New York: Basic Books, 2005).

29 Weigel, *The Cube and the Cathedral*, 2.

30 See further, the report by the Inter-Faith Consultative Group of the Church of England, *Communities and Buildings: Church of England Premises and Other Faiths* (London: Church House Publishing, 1996).

31 Michael Nazir-Ali, *Mission and Dialogue: Proclaiming the Gospel Afresh in Every Age* (London: SPCK, 1995), 101ff.

32 On this in another context, see E.A. Pratt, *Can We Pray with the Unconverted?* (London: CPAS, 1971).

33 For a participant's view, see Robert Runcie's opening address at the 1988 Lambeth Conference in Michael Nazir-Ali and Derek Pattinson (eds.), *The Truth Shall Make You Free:*

The Lambeth Conference, 1988 (London: Church House Publishing, 1994), 21; and the report *Multi-Faith Worship? Questions and Suggestions from the Inter-faith Consultative Group* (London: Church House Publishing, 1992).

34 E.C. Ratcliffe, *The English Coronation Service* (London: SPCK, 1936), 91.

35 For example, by the former President of India, Sarvepalli Radhakrishnan, *The Hindu View of Life* (London: HarperCollins, 1998).

36 See, among others, John Hick (ed.), *Truth and Dialogue: The Relationships between World Religions* (London: Sheldon, 1974); John Hick, *God Has Many Names: Britain's New Religious Pluralism* (London: Macmillan, 1980).

37 R.C. Zaehner, *Mysticism, Sacred and Profane: An Inquiry into Some Varieties of Praeternatural Experience* (Oxford: Oxford University Press, 1957); R.C. Zaehner, *Concordant Discord: Interdependence of Faiths* (Oxford: Oxford University Press, 1970); Iqbal, *Reconstruction of Religious Thought in Islam* (Lahore: Ashaf, 1971), 181ff.

38 Jalāluddīn Rūmī , *Dīwān-i-Shams-i-Tabriz*, Tabriz edn., 1280 AH (Shamsi).

39 See Gavin D'Costa, *Theology and Religious Pluralism* (Oxford: Blackwell, 1986).

2   Who is Jesus? The Unique and Universal Christ

1 N.T. Wright, *Jesus and the Victory of God: Christian Origins and the Question of God* (London: SPCK, 1996), 3ff.

2 See, for example, Jon Sobrino, *Christology at the Crossroads: A Latin American Approach* (London: SCM, 1978); Rene Padilla, 'Christology and Mission in the Two-Thirds World' in Vinay Samuel and Chris Sugden, *Sharing Jesus in the Two-Thirds World* (Bangalore: Partnership in Mission, 1983), 17ff.

3 Kim Yong Bock (ed.), *Minjung Theology: People as the subjects of history* (Singapore: CCA, 1981).

4 Wright, *Jesus and the Victory of God*, 84f.

5 Richard A. Burridge, *Four Gospels, One Jesus: A Symbolic Reading* (London: SPCK, 1994).

6 See on this possible meaning of Luke 17:21, Wright, *Jesus and the Victory of* God, 469.

[7] See further, Hasan Dehqani-Tafti, *Christ and Christianity among the Iranians*, vol. 2 (Basingstoke: Sohrab Books, 1993).

[8] On all of this, see Geoffrey Parrinder, *Jesus in the Qu'Ran*, (Oxford: Oneworld Publications, 1995); Arne Rudvin, 'The Gospel and Islam: What Sort of Dialogue Is Possible?', *al-Mushir*, XXI (Autumn 1979), 314:97ff.

[9] Tarif Khalidi, *The Muslim Jesus: Sayings and Stories in Islamic Literature* (Cambridge, Mass.: Harvard University Press, 2001).

[10] See further, Bill Musk, *Touching the Soul of Islam: Sharing the Gospel in Muslim Countries*, (Crowborough: MARC, 1995).

[11] On this, see James Carleton Paget, 'Jewish proselytism at the time of Christian origins', *Journal for the Study of the New Testament* 62 (1996).

[12] Robert D. Sider, *The Gospel and its Proclamation: Message of the Fathers of the Church* (Wilmington, Del.: Michael Glazier, 1983), 40ff.

[13] Wright, *Jesus and the Victory of God*, 107, 439.

[14] C.K. Barrett, *The New Testament Background: Selected Documents* (London: SPCK, 1961), 166f.

[15] On this, see Colin Hemer, *The Letters to the Seven Churches of Asia in their Local Setting* (London: JSOT Press, Sheffield, 1986).

[16] Bat Ye'or, *The Dhimmi: Jews and Christians under Islam* (London and Toronto: Associated University Presses, 1985), 86f.

[17] Young, *Patriarch, Shah and Caliph*, 23ff.

[18] See Helga Croner, *Stepping Stones to Further Jewish–Christian Relations* and *More Stepping Stones to Further Jewish–Christian Relations* (London and New York: Stimulus Books, 1977 and 1985).

[19] G Vermes, *Jesus the Jew: A Historian's Reading of the Gospels* (London: Collins, 1973); D.Cohn-Sherbok, *On Earth as it is in Heaven: Jews, Christians and Liberation Theology* (Maryknoll, N.Y.: Orbis, 1987); cf. Wright, *Jesus and the Victory of God*, 83ff., 119; and others.

[20] Michael Nazir-Ali, 'The Messianic Idea' in *Common Ground*, Journal of the Council of Christians and Jews (1996), 2:11f.; Pinchas Lapide/Hans Küng, *Brother or Lord? A Jew and a Christian Talk Together about Jesus* (London: Fount, 1977).

21 John Stambaugh and David Balch, *The Social World of the First Christians* (London: SPCK, 1986), 46f.

22 Flannery, *Vatican Council II* (1975), 740.

23 On this, see Michael Nazir-Ali, *Citizens and Exiles: Christian Faith in a Plural World* (London: SPCK, 1998), 22f.; Eric Sharpe, *Not to Destroy but to Fulfil: The Contribution of John Farquhar to Protestant Missionary Thought in India before 1914* (Uppsala: Gleerup, 1965); J.N. Farquhar, *The Crown of Hinduism* (Oxford: Oxford University Press, 1913).

24 For an exposition of this theory as it occurs in *Adversus Haereses*, see J.N.D. Kelly, *Early Christian Doctrines* (London: A&C Black, 1985), 170ff.

25 See Raimundo Pannikar's *The Unknown Christ of Hinduism* (Maryknoll, N.Y.: Orbis, 1981, new edn.).

26 Stanley J. Samartha, *The Hindu Response to the Unbound Christ* (Madras: Christian Literature Society, 1974), 6ff, 19ff, 73ff, 116ff. See also M.M. Thomas, *The Acknowledged Christ of the Indian Renaissance* (London: SCM, 1969).

27 Mission Theological Advisory Group Report, *The Search for Faith*, Introduction and *passim*.

28 Vinoth Ramachandra, *Faiths in Conflict? Christian Integrity in a Multicultural World* (Leicester: Inter-Varsity Press, 1999), 93ff.; cf. B. Witherington III, *Jesus the Sage: The Pilgrimage of Wisdom* (Minneapolis: Fortress, 1994).

29 See further, Elisabeth Schüssler Fiorenza (ed.), *Searching the Scriptures: A Feminist Commentary* (London: SCM, 1995).

30 See C.F.D. Moule, *The Birth of the New Testament* (London: A&C Black, 1966), 63, and his *The Origin of Christology* (Cambridge: Cambridge University Press, 1977); cf. Andy Angel, *Chaos and the Son of Man* (Edinburgh: T&T Clark, 2006), and his unpublished *Like a Bad Penny – The Son of Man, Again!* See also Howard Marshall, 'Jesus Christ, Titles of' in *The Illustrated Bible Dictionary* (Leicester: Inter-Varsity Press, 1980), 773ff.

31 Wright, *Jesus and the Victory of* God, 513f.

32 See further, William Kay and Anne Dyer, *Pentecostal and Charismatic Studies: A Reader* (London: SCM, 2004), 47ff.

33 C.E.B. Cranfield, *The Gospel According to St Mark* (Cambridge: Cambridge University Press, 1966), 336ff.; Wright, *Jesus and the Victory of God*, 579ff.

34   Muhammad Iqbal, *Jāvīd Nāmeh* (Lahore: Ghulam Ali, 1974), 128f.

35   On the whole question of Prophet-veneration, see Michael Nazir-Ali, *Frontiers in Muslim/Christian Encounter* (Oxford: Regnum, 1987), 130ff.

36   See Norberto Saracco, 'The Liberating Options of Jesus' in Samuel and Sugden, *Sharing Jesus in the Two-Thirds World*, 49ff.; Andrew Kirk, *Liberation Theology: An Evangelical View from the Third World* (London: Marshall, Morgan & Scott, 1979), 204f.

37   See, for example, C.E.B. Cranfield, *The Gospel According to St Mark* (Cambridge: Cambridge University Press, 1966), 269ff.

38   Wright, *Jesus and the Victory of God*, 490ff., 554ff.

39   Wright, *Jesus and the Victory of God*, 477f.

40   Ramachandra, *Faiths in Conflict*, 104f.

41   J.D.G. Dunn, *Unity and Diversity in The New Testament: Enquiry into the Character of Earliest Christianity* (London: SCM and Philadelphia: Trinity, 1994), 11ff. See also David Peterson, 'Kerygma or Kerygmata: Is there only one Gospel in the New Testament?' in Chris Green (ed.), *God's Power to Save: One Gospel for a Complex World?* (Leicester: Apollos (Inter-Varsity Press), 2006), 155ff.

42   J.N.D. Kelly, *Early Christian Creeds* (New York: Longman, 19723).

43   See M.R. James, *The Apocryphal New Testament* (Oxford: Clarendon, 1924), 8f.

44   Helmut Koester, *Ancient Christian Gospels: Their History and Development* (London: SCM and Philadelphia, Penn.: Trinity, 1990) 75ff.

45   Koester, *Ancient Christian Gospels*, xxxf.; James, *The Apocryphal New Testament*, xvif.

3   What Does Jesus Do? The Unique and Universal Work

1   F.W. Dillistone, *The Christian Understanding of the Atonement* (Welwyn: Nisbet, 1968), 29ff.

2   See further, Gerhard Von Rad, *Genesis: A Commentary* (London: SCM, 1972), 63f., 98f.

3   See Erev, 'Yom Kippur' in Nosson Scherman et al (eds.), *The Complete Artscroll Siddur* (New York: Mesorah, 1990), 773f.

4   Immanuel Jakobovits in *The Authorised Daily Prayer Book* (St Ives: Singers, 1992), 918ff.

5   Wright, *Jesus and the Victory of* God, 579ff.

6   On the different ways in which this passage has been understood, see A.A. Anderson, *The Book of Psalms*, vol.1, New Century Bible Commentary (London: Marshall, Morgan & Scott, 1972), 314ff.

7   On this, see Hugh Montefiore, *A Commentary on the Epistle to the Hebrews* (London: A&C Black, 1964), 166f.

8   D.A. Carson, *Matthew: Chapters 1 through 12*, Expositor's Bible (Grand Rapids, Zonderman, 1995), 205f.

9   James Allison, *Knowing Jesus* (London: SPCK, 1993).

10 See Gabriel Finaldi, *The Image of Christ* (London: National Gallery, 2000). Numerous anthologies in English also illustrate the centrality of the cross as a classical theme.

11 Ignatius, *Epistle to the Romans* (London: SPCK, 1954) and the Martyrdom of Polycarp in *The Apostolic Fathers* Vol II, Loes Library, Harvard University Press, Cambridge US, 1913, 330.

12 See, for example, Hassan Dehqani-Tafti, *Christ and Christianity among the Iranians*, vols. 1–3 (Basingstoke: Sohrab Books, 1992f.). See also his *Norman Sharpe's Persian Designs* (Basingstoke: Sohrab Books, 2001); Kenneth Cragg, *Jesus and the Muslim: An Exploration* (London: George Allen and Unwin 1985), 41ff.

13 Khalidi, *The Muslim Jesus*, 44.

14 *Mathnawî-i-Ma'navi*, book 2, English trans. E.H.Whinfield (London, 1887), 80–1.

15 Dehqani-Tafti, *Christ and Christianity among the Iranians*, vol. 2, 22; Cragg, *Jesus and the Muslim*, 62.

16 *Kulliyat Awhadī-Isfahānī*, Tehran, Amīr Kabīr, 1340 AH (Shamsi), Eng. trans. A.H. Arberry (London: Classical Persian Literature, 1958), 307–8, 308.

17 Dehqani-Tafti, *Christ and Christianity among the Iranians*, 22; Cragg, *Jesus and the Muslim*, 62f.

18 See further, S. Jeffery, M. Ovey and A. Sach, *Pierced for our Transgressions: Rediscovering the Glory of Penal Substitution* (Nottingham: Inter-Varsity Press, 2007), 271f.

19 On this whole topic, see Oliver O'Donovan's *Resurrection and Moral Order*.

20   Gustaf Aulén, *Christus Victor: An Historical Study of the Three Main Types of the Idea of the Atonement* (London: SPCK, 1950).
21   *Joint Declaration on the Doctrine of Justification* (Grand Rapids: Eerdmans, 2000), 17ff.; cf. *Salvation and the Church, An Agreed Statement by the Anglican-Roman Catholic International Commission* (London: CTS/ACC, 1987); and C. FitzSimons Allison, *The Pastoral and Political Implications of Trent on Justification: A Response to the ARCIC Agreed Statement* , *SLJT*, xxxi (June 1988), 3. See also N.T. Wright, *The New Testament and the People of God* (London: SPCK, 1997), 271f., 298f., 336, 458; and Hans Küng, *Justification: The Doctrine of Karl Barth and a Catholic Reflection* (Philadelphia: Westminster, 1964).
22   Nazir-Ali, *Citizens and Exiles*, 54ff.; Nazir-Ali, *Shapes of the Church to Come* (Eastbourne: Kingsway, 2001), 143ff.
23   See 'Sacrifice and Offering', Richard Bauckham's illuminating passage on this in *The Illustrated Dictionary of the Bible*, Part 3 (Leicester: Inter-Varsity Press, 1980), 358ff.
24   *The Final Report, Eucharistic Doctrine, Elucidation* (London: CTS/SPCK, 1982), 21.

4   Lord of All: Christ, Culture and Context

1   See further, Charles H. Kraft, *Christianity in Culture: A Study in Biblical Theologizing in Cross Cultural Perspective* (Maryknoll, N.Y.: Orbis,1979), 45ff.; and Eugen Nunnemacher, 'Culture' in Karl Müller, Theo Sundermeier and Stephen B. Bevans (eds.), *Dictionary of Mission: Theology, History, Perspectives* (Maryknoll, N.Y.: Orbis, 1997), 94f.
2   Flannery, *Vatican Council II* (1988), 958f.
3   On the relation between these, see James Ward, *The Realm of Ends: Pluralism and Theism* (Cambridge: Cambridge University Press, 1912).
4   John Henry Newman, *Apologia Pro Vita Sua* (London: Fontana, 1959), 278.
5   Kraft, *Christianity in Culture*,169f., 345f.
6   I. Howard Marshall, *The Acts of the Apostles* (Leicester: Inter-Varsity Press, 1984), 283ff.
7   See further, Sider, *The Gospel and its Proclamation*, 40ff.
8   C.F.D. Moule, *The Epistles to the Colossians and to Philemon* (Cambridge: Cambridge University Press, 1957), 126f.

9   Sider, *The Gospel and its Proclamation*, 77.
10 Rudvin, 'The Gospel and Islam', 111f.
11 Sider, *The Gospel and its Proclamation*, 77, 66f., 90, et al.
12 Michael Nazir-Ali, *Citizens and* Exiles,116; Young, *Patriarch, Shah and Caliph*, 15f.
13 Rudvin, 'The Gospel and Islam', 112f.
14 Karl Barth and Emil Brunner, P. Fraenkel (tr.), *Natural Theology* (London: Bles, 1946). See also Michael Banner, *Christian Ethics and Contemporary Moral Problems* (Cambridge: Cambridge University Press, 1999), 281f.; Oliver O'Donovan, *Resurrection and Moral Order*, 76f.
15 H. Richard Niebuhr, *Christ and Culture* (London: Faber & Faber, 1952).
16 Lamin Sanneh, *Translating the Message: The Missionary Impact on Culture* (Maryknoll, N.Y.: Orbis, 1989).
17 David Gitari, 'Evangelisation and Culture' in Vinay Samuel and Albrecht Hauser (eds.), *Proclaiming Christ in Christ's Way: Studies in Integral Evangelism (Oxford: Regnum, 1989), 101ff.*
18 See further Francis Murphy, *The Christian Way of Life: Message of the Fathers of the Church* (Wilmington, Del.: Michael Glazier, 1986).
19 Lamin Sanneh, *Translating the Message*; Lamin Sanneh, *Whose Religion is Christianity?:The Gospel Beyond the West* (Grand Rapids: Eerdmans, 2003).
20 Joseph Ratzinger, 'Christ, Faith and the Challenge of Cultures', *Origins* 24 (30 March 1995), no. 41.
21 Pope Benedict XVI, *Faith, Reason and the University: Memories and Reflections* (Vatican Library, September 2006).
22 Michael Nazir-Ali, *Islam: A Christian Perspective* (Exeter: Paternoster, 1983), 66f.; Michael Nazir-Ali, *Frontiers in Muslim–Christian Encounter* (Oxford: Regnum, 1987), 15 and *passim*; R. Walzer, *Greek into Arabic* (Oxford: Oxford University Press, 1962); Morris S. Seale, *Muslim Theology: A Study of Origins with Reference to the Church Fathers* (London: Luzac, 1964).
23 Young, *Patriarch, Shah and Caliph*, 3ff.
24 See particularly the introduction to St Athanasius, *On the Incarnation* (London: Mowbray, 1982), 18ff.

25   See further, Margaret Smith, *Studies in Early Mysticism in the Near and Middle-East* (Oxford: Oneworld Publications, 1995); Muhammad Iqbal, *The Development of Metaphysics in Persia* (Lahore: Bazm-i-iqbal, 1964), 76ff.; Benedicta Ward, *The Sayings of the Desert Fathers* (London: Mowbray, 1981); Laura Swan, *The Forgotten Desert Mothers: Sayings, Lives and Stories of Early Christian Women* (New York: Paulist Press, 2001).

26   Henry Hill (ed.), *Light from the East: A Symposium on the Oriental, Orthodox and Assyrian Churches* (Toronto: Syrian Book Centre, 1988).

27   Stephen Neill and Owen Chadwick, *The Penguin History of the Church: History of Christian Missions*, vol. 6 (London: Penguin, 1992), 197f.

28   See C. Peter Williams, ' "Not Transplanting": Henry Venn's Strategic Vision' in Kevin Ward and Brian Stanley (eds.) *The Church Mission Society and World Christianity 1799–1999* (Richmond: Curzon, 2000), 147ff.; also Peter Williams, *The Ideal of the Self-governing Church: A Study in Victorian Missionary Strategy* (Leiden: Brill, 1990).

29   Roland Allen, *Missionary Methods: St Paul's or Ours?* (Cambridge: Lutterworth, 2006); *The Spontaneous Expansion of the Church: And the Causes Which Hinder It* (Cambridge: Lutterworth, 2006).

30   Philip Jenkins, *The Next Christendom: The Coming of Global Christianity* (New York: Oxford University Press USA, 2002) 69f.

31   C.O. Buchanan, *Modern Anglican Liturgies 1958–1968* (Oxford: Oxford University Press, 1968), 25f.; cf. the present author's preparatory paper for the Lambeth Conference 1988, 'Liturgical Development in the Anglican Communion: A View' (March 1988).

32   Stephen Neill, *A History of Christian Missions* (London: Penguin, 1986), 138ff., 156ff. See also, Nazir-Ali, *From Everywhere to Everywhere: A World View of Christian Mission* (London: Collins, 1990), 82, 154.

33   For a critique, see the Lausanne Occasional Paper No.1, *The Pasadena Consultation – Homogeneous Unit Principle* (Wheaton: Lausanne Committee for World Evangelization, 1978).

[34] Michael Nazir-Ali, *Islam: A Christian Perspective* (Exeter: Paternoster, 1983); cf. Phil Parshall, *Beyond the Mosque: Christians within Muslim Community* (Grand Rapids: Baker, 1985), 188f.

[35] On this issue, see *Women Bishops in the Church of England?: A Report of the House of Bishops' Working Party on Women in the Episcopate* (London: Church House Publishing, 2004), 161ff.

[36] E.g. Ignatius, *Epistle to the Ephesians*, 20:2 (London: SPCK, 1984); Justin, *First Apology*, 65–67 in Joseph Lienhard, *Ministry: Message of the Fathers of the Church* (Wilmington, Del.: Michael Glazier, 1984), 36f.

[37] See further, Michael Nazir-Ali, *Shapes of the Church to Come* (Eastbourne: Kingsway, 2001), 71ff.

[38] Michael Nazir-Ali, *From Everywhere to Everywhere*, 38ff.

[39] Ephraim Radner and Philip Turner, *The Fate of Communion: The Agony of Anglicanism and the Future of a Global Church* (Grand Rapids: Eerdmans, 2006).

[40] Samuel M. Zwemer, *The Moslem Christ* (New York: American Tract Society, 1912), 183.

[41] For an example of the former position, see Parshall, *Beyond the Mosque*, and of the latter, Paul-Gordon Chandler, *Pilgrims of Christ on the Muslim Road: Exploring a New Path between Two Faiths* (Lanham, Md.: Rowman and Littlefield, 2007).

5 'Not far from any one of us': Christ and the Religions

[1] On all of this, see further my *Conviction and Conflict*, 7ff.

[2] See Maurice Cowling, *Religion and Public Doctrine in England*, vols. 1–3 (Cambridge: Cambridge University Press, 2004).

[3] See, for example, Kenneth W. Jones, *Socio-Religious Reform Movements in British India*, The New Cambridge History of India (Cambridge: Cambridge University Press, 1989).

[4] On this, see further, Norman Gottwald, *The Tribes of Yahweh: A Sociology of the Religion of Liberated Israel 1250–1050 BCE* (Maryknoll, N.Y.: Orbis, 1979), 611ff.; John Goldingay, *Theological Diversity and the Authority of the Old Testament* (Grand Rapids: Eerdmans, 1987), 66f.

[5] Goldingay, *Theological Diversity*, 68, 153; Robert A.J. Gagnon, *The Bible and Homosexual Practice: Texts and Hermeneutics* (Nashville: Abingdon Press, 2001), 43ff.

6   Gerhard Von Rad, *Genesis: A Commentary* (London: SCM, 1972), 179f.

7   On this, see Donald Wiseman, *I and II Kings* (Leicester: Inter-Varsity Press, 1993), 97ff.

8   Goldingay, *Theological Diversity*, 69f.

9   See further, Norman Habel, *The Book of Job* (London: SCM, 1985), 39f.; H.H. Rowley, *The Book of Job* (Grand Rapids: Eerdmans, 1980), 23f.

10 See Leslie Allen, *The Books of Joel, Obadiah, Jonah and Micah* (Grand Rapids: Eerdmans, 1976), 175ff.

11 See further, Robert A. Anderson, *Signs and Wonders: A Commentary on the Book of Daniel* (Grand Rapids: Eerdmans, 1984), 39ff.

12 Claus Westermann, *Isaiah 40–66* (London: SCM, 1969), 152 ff.

13 See Young, *Patriarch, Shah and Caliph*, 3.

14 On all this, see Kenneth Cracknell, *Towards a New Relationship* (London, Epworth, 1986), 27ff.

15 J.B. Lightfoot, *Saint Paul's Epistle to the Philippians* (London: Macmillan, 1903), 270ff.

16 See further, Howard Marshall, *The Acts of the Apostles* (Leicester: Inter-Varsity Press, 1984), 281ff.

17 Sider, *The Gospel and its Proclamation*, 73ff.

18 Cracknell, *Towards a New Relationship*, 29.

19 Rudvin, *The Gospel and Islam*, 109f.

20 Nazir-Ali, *Citizens and Exiles*, 131f.; cf. Nazir-Ali, *Mission and Dialogue*, 77f.

21 Cracknell, *Towards a New Relationship*, 50; cf. Joyce Baldwin, *Haggai, Zechariah and Malachi* (London: Tyndale, 1972), 227ff.

22 See further, Otto Kaiser, *Isaiah 13–39* (London: SCM, 1980), 104ff.

23 Nazir-Ali, *Citizens and Exiles*, 133f.

24 Nazir-Ali, *Mission and Dialogue*,111ff.

25 John V. Taylor, *The Go-Between God: The Holy Spirit and Christian Mission* (London: SCM, 1972), 42ff.

26 Georges Khodr, 'Christianity in a Pluralistic World – The Economy of the Holy Spirit' in Constantine G. Patelos (ed.), *The Orthodox Church in the Ecumenical Movement: Documents and Statements, 1902–75* (Geneva: World Council of Churches, 1978), 297ff.

27 V. Lossky, *Essai sur la Theologie Mystique de l'Eglise d'Orient* (Paris: Aubier, 1944), 156. See also Khodr, *Christianity in a Pluralistic World*, 305.

28 See further, *Beyond the Impasse: Towards a Pneumatological Theology of Religions* (Grand Rapids: Baker, and Carlisle: Paternoster, 2003). See also, Allan Anderson, *An Introduction to Pentecostalism: Global Charismatic Christianity* (Cambridge: Cambridge University Press, 2004), 202f., 283.

29 R.C. Zaehner, *Our Savage God* (London: Collins, 1974), 9ff.; Richard L. Schebera, *Christian, Non-Christian Dialogue: The Vision of Robert C. Zaehner* (Washington: University Press of America, 1978), 88ff.

6 The Unique and Universal Mission

1 See Howard Marshall, *The Gospel of Luke: A Commentary on the Greek Text* (Exeter: Paternoster, 1978), 412f.

2 Allen, *Missionary Methods*, 76, 83, 95ff.

3 On the question of Jewish witness in a Gentile environment, see J. Carlton Paget, 'Jewish Proselytism at the Time of Christian Origins', *JSNT* 62 (1996), 65ff.

4 On folk religion, see the Mission Theological Advisory Group report, *The Search for Faith*, 45 ff.

5 On this, see my *Shapes of the Church to Come*, 103ff. and the report from the Mission and Public Affairs Council of the Church of England, *Mission-Shaped Church* (London: Church House Publishing, 2004).

6 Robert Eno, *Teaching Authority in the Early Church* (Wilmington, Del.: Michael Glazier, 1984), 91; Joseph Lienhard, *Ministry: Message of the Fathers of the Church* (Wilmington, Del.: Michael Glazier, 1984), 136f.; Henry Chadwick, *The Early Church* (London: Penguin, 1967), 133ff., 219ff.

7 See further, Karl Rahner's essay 'Broadening the Classical Concept of Martyrdom', in Brian Wicker (ed.), *Witnesses to Faith?: Martyrdom in Christianity and Islam* (Aldershot: Ashgate, 2006), 147ff.

8 *Christian Martyrs of the Twentieth Century* (London: Westminster Abbey, July 1998), 1. For an account of the martyrs' lives and deaths, see Andrew Chandler and Anthony Harvey (eds.), *The Terrible Alternative: Christian*

Martyrdom in the Twentieth Century (London: Cassell, 1998).

9   Rahner, 'Broadening the Classical Concept of Martyrdom', 148.

10 Peter C. Phan, *Social Thought: Message of the Fathers of the Church* (Wilmington, Del.: Michael Glazier, 1984), 21f.

11 E.A. Judge, 'Cultural Conformity and Innovation in Paul: Some clues from contemporary documents', Tyndale Bulletin 35 (1984), 6; Moule, *The Epistles to the Colossians and to Philemon*, 126ff.

12 Stambaugh and Balch, *The Social World of the First Christians*, 54f, 141, etc.; Murphy, *The Christian Way of Life*, 20.

13 Peter Phan, *Social Thought*, 122ff, 135ff. See also Donald Winslow, 'Gregory of Nazianzus and Love for the Poor' in *Anglican Theological Review*, XLVII (October 1965), 4:348ff.

14 See further Dale Irvin and Scott Sunquist, *History of the World Christian Movement*, vol. 1 (Maryknoll, N.Y.: Orbis, 2003), 423ff.

15 David Bebbington, *Evangelicalism in Modern Britain* (London: Unwin, 1989), 105ff.

16 Bebbington, *Evangelicalism in Modern Britain*, 263f.; and the Grand Rapids Report, *Evangelism and Social Responsibility: An Evangelical Commitment*, by the Lausanne Committee for World Evangelization and the World Evangelical Fellowship (Exeter: Paternoster, 1982), 24.

17 There is now a vast literature but see, for example, Vinay Samuel and Albrecht Hauser, *Proclaiming Christ in Christ's Way: Studies in Integral Evangelism* (Oxford: Regnum, 1989); and the collection *Mission as Transformation: A Theology of the Whole Gospel* edited by Vinay Samuel and Chris Sugden (Oxford: Regnum, 1999).

18 Such an agenda is seen, for instance, in the movement's journal on mission and ethics: *Transformation*.

19 See Nazir-Ali, *Mission and Dialogue*, 60; Bebbington, *Evangelicalism in Modern Britain*, 211f.; cf. 'Justice' in *The Dictionary of the Ecumenical Movement* (Geneva: World Council of Churches, 1991), 554f.

20 For the origins of liberation theology, see Andrew Kirk, *Liberation Theology: An Evangelical View from the Third World* (London: Marshall, Morgan & Scott, 1979), 23ff. For the

ecclesial aspect, see Leonardo Boff, *Ecclesiogenesis: The Base Communities Reinvent the Church* (London: Collins, 1986).

21 David Martin, *Pentecostalism: The World Their Parish* (Oxford: Blackwell, 2002).

22 On all of this, see Nazir-Ali, *From Everywhere to Everywhere*, 162ff.

23 See further, Nazir-Ali, *Mission and Dialogue*, 59ff. See also my *Conviction and Conflict*, 139ff.

24 For the ecumenical discussion, see Nazir-Ali, *From Everywhere to Everywhere*,162ff., and *Citizens and Exiles*, 135f.

25 See further, Pontifical Council for Inter-Religious Dialogue, 'Dialogue and Proclamation', *The Bulletin*, issue 26 (May 1991), 2:42f.

26 *Evangelism and Social Responsibility*, 23.

27 Kenneth Bailey, *Poet and Peasant and Through Peasant Eyes: A Literary-Cultural Approach to the Parables in Luke* (Grand Rapids: Eerdmans, 1985), 173f.

28 J.N.D. Anderson, *Christianity and Comparative Religion* (Leicester: Inter-Varsity Press, 1970); *God's Law and God's Love* (London: Collins, 1980); cf. Cracknell, *Towards a New Relationship*, 53ff.

29 Michael Nazir-Ali, *Mission and Dialogue*,13ff.

30 Nazir-Ali, *Citizens and Exiles*, 36, 80, 118.

31 Nazir-Ali, *Mission and Dialogue*, 23.

32 John V. Taylor, *The Go-Between God*, 178ff.

33 For example, see Kenneth Cragg, *To Meet and to Greet: Faith with Faith* (London: Epworth, 1992), 43f., 126ff.

34 See further, Samartha, *The Hindu Response to the Unbound Christ*, 122ff.

35 See, for example, Parshall, *Beyond the Mosque*.

36 Chandler, *Pilgrims of Christ on the Muslim Road*.

37 Parshall, *Beyond the Mosque*, 180f.

38 Parshall, *Beyond the Mosque*, 193f.

Select Bibliography

Aulén, Gustaf, *Christ as Victor: An Historical Study of the Three Main Types of the Idea of the Atonement* (London, SPCK, 1950).

Allen, Roland, *Missionary Methods: St Paul's or Ours?* (Cambridge, Lutterworth, 2006).

Allison, James, *Knowing Jesus* (London, SPLK, 1993).

Anderson, J.N.D., *Christianity and Comparative Religion,* Leicester (IVP, 1970).

Bailey, Kenneth, *Poet and Peasant and Through Peasant Eyes: A Literary–Cultural Approach to the Parables in Luke* (Grand Rapids, Eerdmans, 1985).

Bebbington, David, *Evangelicalism in Modern Britain* (London, Unwin, 1989).

Biggar, Nigel, *Aiming to Kill: The Ethics of Suicide and Euthanasia* (London, DLT, 2004).

Burridge, Richard, *Four Gospels, One Jesus: A Symbolic Reading* (London, SPCK, 1994).

Chandler, Andrew and Harvey, Anthony (eds), *The Terrible Alternative: Christian Martyrdom in the 20th Century* (London, Cassell, 1998).

Cowling, Maurice, *Religion and Public Doctrine in England,* Vols. 1–3 (Cambridge, CUP, 2004).

Cracknell, Kenneth, *Towards a New Relationship: Christians and People of Other Faith* (London, Epworth, 1986).

Cragg, Kenneth, *To Meet and to Greet: Faith with Faith* (London, Epworth, 1992).

Cromartie, Michael (ed.), *A Presuming Grace: Protestants, Catholics and Natural Law* (Grand Rapids, Eerdmans/EPPC, 1997).

D'Costa, Gavin, *Theology and Religious Pluralism* (Oxford, Blackwell, 1986).

Dillistone, F.W. *The Christian Understanding of the Atonement* (Welwyn, Nisbet, 1968).

Dunn, J.D.G., *Unity and Diversity in the New Testament: Enquiry into the Character of Earliest Christianity* (London, SCM and Philadelphia: Trinity, 1994).

Farquhar, J. N., *The Crown of Hinduism* (Oxford, OUP, 1913).

Goldingay, John, *Theological Diversity and the Authority of the Old Testament* (Grand Rapids, Eardmans, 1987).

Gordon-Chandler, Paul, *Pilgrims of Christ on the Muslim Road: Exploring a New Path between Two Faiths* (Lanham, MD, Rowsman and Littlefield, 2007).

Habgood, John, *Confessions of a Conservative Liberal* (London, SPCK, 1988).

Jenkins, Philip, *The Next Christendom: The Coming of Global Christianity* (New York, OUP, 2002).

Khalidi, Tarif, *The Muslim Jesus: Sayings and Stories in Islamic Literature* (Cambridge, Mass, Harvard University Press, 2001).

Kraft, Charles, *Christianity in Culture: A Study in Biblical Theologizing in Cross Cultural Perspective* (Maryknoll, N.Y., Orbis, 1997).

MacIntyre, Alasdair, *After Virtue: A Study in Moral Theory* (London, Duckworth, 2000).

Martin, David, *Pentecostalism: The World Their Parish* (Oxford, Blackwell, 2002).

Marty, Martin, *When Faiths Collide* (Oxford, Blackwell, 2005).

MTAG, *The Search for Faith and the Witness of the Church* (London, CHP, 1996).

Neill, Stephen and Chadwick, Owen, *The Penguin History of the Church: History of Christian Missions*, Vol. 6 (London, Penguin, 1992).

Niebuhr, Richard H. *Christ and Culture* (London, Faber and Faber, 1952).

O'Donovan, Oliver, *Resurrection and Moral Order: An Outline for Evangelical Ethics* (Leicester, IVP, 1986).

Pannikar, Raimundo, *The Unknown Christ of Hinduism* (Maryknoll, NY, Orbis, 1981), new ed.

Phan, Peter, *Social Thought: Message of the Fathers of the Church* (Wilmington, Del, Michael Glazier, 1984).

Ramachandra, Vinoth, *Faiths in Conflict? Christian Integrity in a Multicultural World* (Leicester, IVP, 1999).

Samartha, Stanley, *The Hindu Response to the Unbound Christ* (Madras, Christian Literature Society, 1974).

Samuel, Vinay and Sugden, Christopher, *Sharing Jesus in the Two-Thirds World* (Bangalore, PIM, 1983).

Sanneh, Lamin, *Translating the Message: The Missionary Impact on Culture* (Maryknoll, N.Y., Orbis, 1989).

Sider, Robert D., *The Gospel and its Proclamation: Message of the Fathers of the Church* (Wilmington, Del; Michael Glazier, 1983).

Smith, Margaret, *Studies in Early Mysticism in the Near and Middle East* (Oxford, Oneworld, 1995).

Sobrino, Jon, *Christology at the Crossroads: A Latin American Approach* (London, SCM, 1978).

Song, Robert, *Human Genetics: Fabricating the Future* (London, DLT, 2002).

Stambaugh, John and Balch, David, *The Social World of the First Christians* (London, SPCK, 1986).

Taylor, John V., *The Go-Between God: The Holy Spirit and Christian Mission (London, SCM, 1972).*

Thomas, M.M., *The Acknowledged Christ of the Indian Renaissance* (London, SCM, 1969).

Vermes, G, *Jesus the Jew: A Historian's Reading of the Gospels* (London, Collins, 1973).

Weigel, George, *The Cube and the Cathedral: Europe, America and Politics Without God.*

Wright, N.T., *Jesus and the Victory of God: Christian Origins and the Question of God* (London, SPCK, 1996).

Wright, N.T., *The New Testament and the People of God* (London, SPCK, 1997).

Zaehner, R.C. *Mysticism, Sacred and Profane: An Inquiry into Some Varieties of Praeternatural Experience* (Oxford, OUP, 1957).

Zwemer, Samuel, *The Moslem Christ* (New York, American Tract Society, 1912).

Some of the author's books:

Conviction and Conflict: *Islam, Christianity and World Order* (Continuum, 2006).

Understanding My Muslim Neighbour [with Chris Stone] (Canterbury Press, 2002).

Shapes of the Church to Come (Kingsway, Eastbourne, 2001).

Citizens and Exiles: *Christian Faith in a Plural Society* (SPCK, London 1998, United Church Press, Cleveland, 1998).

The Mystery of Faith (CFS, Lahore, 1995).

Mission and Dialogue: *Proclaiming the Gospel Afresh in Every Age* (SPCK, London, 1995).

From Everywhere to Everywhere: *A World View of Christian Mission* (Collins, London, 1990).

Frontiers in Christian-Muslim Encounter (Regnum, Oxford 1987).

Islam, a Christian Perspective (Paternoster Press, Exeter 1982, (Westminster Press, Philadelphia, 1983).

Index of Biblical, Deutero-Canonical and Qur'ānic References

Index

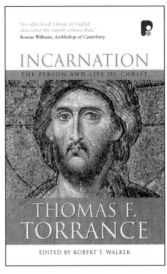

'No other book I know in English does what this superb volume does.'
Rowan Williams, Archbishop of Canterbury

Incarnation

The Person and Life of Christ

Thomas F. Torrence
(edited by Robert T. Walker)

Thomas F. Torrance's new book on Christology combines heart and head in a deeply biblical, unified, Christ-centred and Trinitarian theology. It presents a full account of the meaning and significance of the life and person of Jesus Christ, arguing that his work of revelation and reconciliation can only be understood in the light of who he is (real God and real man united in one person). Torrance argues that the whole life of Jesus Christ – from his birth, through his ministry, cross, resurrection, and ascension to his second coming – is of saving significance.

"No other book I know in English does what this superb volume does in presenting with absolute clarity the full classical doctrine of the universal church on the person and work of Christ. It is a wonderful legacy from one of the very greatest English-language systematic theologians." – **Rowan Williams**, Archbishop of Canterbury

Thomas F. Torrance MBE (1913-2007) served for 27 years as Professor of Christian Dogmatics at New College, Edinburgh and was the author of many academic books and articles. **Robert T. Walker**, nephew of T.F. Torrance, studied theology (with his uncle) and philosophy. He now divides his time between teaching theology at Edinburgh University and teaching outdoor pursuits.

978-1-84227-607-5

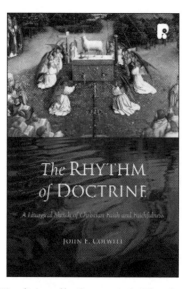

The Rhythm of Doctrine

A Liturgical Sketch of Christian Faith and Faithfulness

John E. Colwell

Traditionally Systematic Theology is structured around the articles of the Creed: the doctrine of God, the doctrine of Christ, the doctrine of the Spirit, the doctrine of the Church, and so on. Whilst this approach has its benefits it is not without flaws. One weakness is that the roots and context of theology in Christian *worship* can be lost sight of and discussions can become abstract and disconnected from the life of faith. But there is another way to structure Systematic Theology, an approach more explicitly and self-consciously rooted in the rhythm of the liturgy followed by most Christians for most of the years of the Church's history.

In *The Rhythm of Doctrine* John Colwell provides a short, inspiring introduction to a Systematic Theology that is built around the worshipful rhythms of the Christian Year. Chapters include the One who comes (Advent); the One who takes our humanity (Christmas); the One who is revealed (Epiphany); the one who journeys to the cross (Lent); the One who lives and reigns (Easter); the One who indwells and transforms (Pentecost); and the One who invites us into communion ('All Saints Day'). In this ancient-future way Christian worship, theology and discipleship are woven into a seamless garment.

John E. Colwell is Tutor in Christian Doctrine and Ethics at Spurgeon's College, London. He is author of *Promise and Presence* and *Living in the Christian Story*.

978-1-84227-498-9

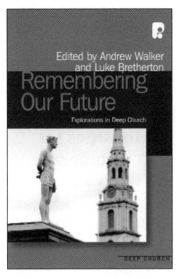

Remembering Our Future

Explorations in Deep Church

Edited by Andrew Walker and Luke Bretherton

Many are exasperated with what they perceive as the fad-driven, one-dimensional spirituality of modern evangelicalism. Instead they desire to reconnect with, and be deeply rooted in, the common historical Christian tradition as well as their evangelical heritage: Welcome to what C.S. Lewis called 'Deep Church'. At its heart Deep Church is about remembering our past in order to face our future. *Remembering Our Future* raises some very compelling questions for both emerging and inherited church leaders as it offers a new vision of living traditions of worship, discipleship and service. One of the most important questions this thoughtful book asks is, 'How can we both listen to the wisdom of ages past and be open to the on-going creative work of God today?'

> 'These essays are the best attempt I have come across to address the emerging church's need for a deep ecclesiology. I not only recommend a rigorous contemplation of this book, but also commend its vision of "Deep Church" as a worthy goal for all streams of church life. – **Andrew Jones**, tallskinnykiwi.com and Missional Cell Developer, Church Mission Society

Andrew Walker is Professor of Theology and Education at King's College London and an ecumenical canon of St Paul's Cathedral. **Luke Bretherton** is Lecturer in Theology and Ministry, Convener of the Faith and Public Policy Forum and DMin Programme Director at King's College London.

978-1-84227-504-7

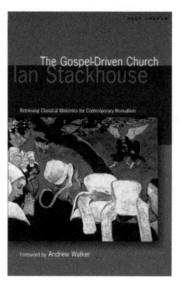

The Gospel-Driven Church

Retrieving Classical Ministries for Contemporary Revivalism

Ian Stackhouse

Charismatic Renewal has at the core of its ideology an aspiration for revival. This is a laudable aspiration, but in recent years, in the absence of large-scale evangelistic impact, such a vision has encouraged a faddist mentality among many Charismatic church leaders.

The Gospel-Driven Church documents this development and the numerous theological and pastoral distortions that take place when genuine revival fervour transmutes into revivalism. Ian Stackhouse shows how a retrieval of some of the core practices of the church – preaching, the sacraments, the laying on of hands and prayer – are essential at this moment in the Charismatic Renewal. He commends a recovery of the classical 'means of grace' as a way of keeping the church centred on the gospel rather than on mere concerns about numbers.

> 'A model of careful biblical and spiritual discernment, both appreciative and cautionary. I find him a most welcome ally in our "stay against confusion".' – **Eugene Peterson**, Professor Emeritus of Spiritual Theology, Regent College, Vancouver BC, Canada

Ian Stackhouse is Pastoral Leader of Guildford Baptist Church, UK.

978-1-84227-290-9

Public Theology in Cultural Engagement

edited by
Stephen Holmes

Public Theology in Cultural Engagement offers foundational and programmatic essays exploring helpful ways to theologise about culture with missional intent. The book opens with three chapters taking steps towards developing a general theology of culture. Part Two explores the contribution of key biblical themes to a theology of culture – creation, law, election, Christology, and redemption. The final section considers theological proposals for engagement with culture past and present with contemporary reflections on nationalism and on drug culture. Contributors include Colin Gunton, Robert Jenson, Stephen Holmes, Colin Greene, Luke Bretherton and Brian Horne.

'This book represents groundbreaking and foundational thinking.' – **David Spriggs**, The Bible Society UK

Stephen R. Holmes is a Baptist minister and Lecturer in Theology at the University of St Andrews in Scotland.

978-1-84227-542-9

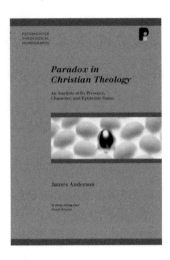

Paradox in Christian Theology

An Analysis of Its Presence, Character, and Epistemic Status

James Anderson

Does traditional creedal Christianity involve paradoxical doctrines, that is, doctrines which present the appearance (at least) of logical inconsistency? If so, what is the nature of these paradoxes and why do they arise? What is the relationship between 'paradox' and, 'mystery' in theological theorizing? And what are the implications for the rationality, or otherwise, of orthodox Christian beliefs? In *Paradox in Christian Theology*, James Anderson argues that the doctrines of the Trinity and the Incarnation, as derived from Scripture and formulated in the ecumenical creeds, are indeed paradoxical. But this conclusion, he contends, need not imply that Christians who believe these doctrines are irrational in doing so. In support of this claim, Anderson develops and defends a model of understanding paradoxical Christian doctrines according to which the presence of such doctrines is unsurprising and adherence to paradoxical doctrines can be entirely reasonable. As such, the phenomenon of theological paradox cannot be considered as a serious intellectual obstacle to belief in Christianity. The case presented in this book has significant implications for the practice of systematic theology, biblical exegesis, and Christian apologetics.

'In defending the ineluctable presence of paradox in theology, James Anderson argues that attempts to avoid this will result in formulations that are inadequate to the articulation of core Christian doctrines. What is particularly striking about this study is its accomplished engagement of important recent work in analytic philosophy of religion.' – **David Fergusson**, University of Edinburgh

978-1-84227-462-0